Lady Don't Fall Backwards

Joan Le Mesurier

Lady Don't Fall Backwards

PAN BOOKS
London, Sydney and Auckland

First published in Great Britain 1988 by Sidgwick & Jackson Ltd
This edition published 1989 by Pan Books Ltd,
Cavaye Place, London SW10 9PG
9 8 7 6 5 4 3 2 1
© Joan Le Mesurier 1988
ISBN 0 330 30994 3

Photoset by Parker Typesetting Service, Leicester
Printed and bound in Great Britain by
Richard Clay Limited, Bungay, Suffolk

To my husband John

Acknowledgements

To my mother, for having the courage to always be herself. Her wisdom and her strength reveal themselves to me increasingly with every day that passes. To Derek Taylor, for his epilogue and for staying 'connected'. To my son David, for his enthusiasm and encouragement, his devotion to John and Tony, and for seeing things as they really were. To my agent, Gill Coleridge, for finding Susan Hill, who pushed me the last half mile. To Sue Hogg, who blew away the chaff. To Mark, for never going far away. To Diana Eden, who knows about writing and mixes her ink with brains. And lastly, to my granddaughter, Emma, who I really wrote it for, because she loves 'Ganga''s stories, with added thanks to her mother, Susie, who gave me my most precious gift.

Contents

Prologue

I am a great believer in fate. There are some things that lie in wait for us with our name on them. There are some people who, from the first time we meet them, seem to fit like familiar old friends. The moment my son David was first put into my arms, I said, through the mists of analgesia, 'I know that face.' It was the same with my first husband, Mark Eden – I knew at once who he was. On meeting John Le Mesurier, who was to become my second husband, I felt as if I had put on a comfortable old coat. But in the case of Tony Hancock, I experienced a shock of recognition.

Coming as I do from the 'who's going to look at you?' school of thought, I graduated naturally with the belief that if anyone looked at me at all I would be lucky. I spent most of my formative years trying to make people not only look at me, but like what they saw. It was not until quite recently that I took a good look at myself. Armed with a massive lack of self-confidence, I had been under the illusion that everybody out there knew something I did not, that they were in on some joke that I had failed to understand. However, in spite of this handicap, I always found I was drawn intuitively towards certain people and away from others.

In this respect I have seldom been wrong, except for a few expensive mistakes made, I hasten to add, in a deliberate attempt to hurl myself lemming-like at life. In short, I was a pushover. The surest way of getting me into bed was a well-timed line, and the sexiest thing about a man has always been his sense of humour.

As for me, looking back at my life, I know that without a sense of humour there were times when I might have gone under. The funniest thing of all is sometimes the hardest thing to laugh at, namely, oneself.

One

Spring is definitely on its way. The clump of daffodils planted in the autumn has broken through the earth to a height of six inches, in spite of the gallons of cats' pee poured over it during the winter months and the many attempts to uproot the young bulbs and replace them with hard black turds. There they stand triumphant, living proof that yet another of the English things I love and thought I would miss is flourishing along with me in this alien soil where I too am putting down new and tentative roots and feeling them catch and take hold.

I first spotted the cottage because of the cats. About four or five of them were skulking about, so I went down to investigate, thinking that the pretty little street went through to the beach. And there at the end of it was the cottage. Well, not quite at the end; there was another one nestling against it, of the same period, slightly different in design, equally pretty. Both cottages had plants in tubs on their windowsills and across the street each had a small garden no more than a yard wide, backed by a high stone wall. Trees, mostly pepper trees, grew right down the length of the street and against the wall were creeping plants – ivy, morning glory, roses. Right opposite what was eventually to become my cottage was a palm tree whose branches reached across the little lane and rested on the upper windowsills. Total enchantment, and cats to boot.

A woman came out of the cottage, friendly and smiling. She turned out to be an American, a writer studying parapsychology. She had lived there for a year and was soon to go home. She was 'all Spained out', she said, tired of living primitively. Strange things had happened in the cottage, she told me, lots of strong energy. She had sorted herself out there. I stepped over the threshold and into her shoes – I had a lot of sorting out to do and this seemed the very place in which to do it.

The first winter has passed. The only strange things that have happened are that the lights frequently fuse and I am happy. If I had known a few years before that within a short space of time I would lose my husband, my father, a hell of a lot of 'friends', who departed with John, the lovely house with the big gardens, the security of a good income, even my beloved cats, one of whom was nineteen years old, and that I would be living alone in a tiny cottage, cooking in brackish water, with a log fire for heat and the daily penance of a feeble shower in an icy tiled bathroom, I think I would have wanted to give the whole thing up there and then.

The fact that I have come through at all seems like a miracle. That I have come through and am happy is very strange indeed. Of course, the sadness is still there lying dormant, and the memories pop into the mind at unguarded moments, in those wicked wee small hours, for example. But they come with nothing like the frequency with which they occurred back home in England, where everything around me had a history and every street led me back into the past. The hospital where John died, a godsend being so near during his illness, an ordeal to pass every day afterwards; the harbour that Dad loved, worked on, fished from, fell in and escaped to for peace and quiet, no joy for me to walk around now; my garden, which always gave me a deep sense of tranquillity, a sad place without the company of the cats and the sight of John seated in the window of his study, learning his lines or writing at his desk. Every wall, every drawer, cupboard, shelf and chair, every painting, ornament, photograph and wardrobe held a memory. It seemed to me that everything good was over and that I was the keeper of a museum.

One day I gave myself a good talking to. 'With a bit of luck,' I said, 'you still have a third of your life left. Why don't you try to make it the best bit.' So I sold the house and came to Spain for a holiday, by which time John had been dead for a year and a half and Dad for four months. Mother was coping well; she was adjusting to widowhood and, to be honest, while not exactly enjoying herself, she was experiencing the relief which comes when the years of watching someone you love suffer are at an end and the accompanying exhaustion which was pushed into the background for so long, is over. She was, and still is, an active, youthful woman, looking much nearer her mid-sixties than approaching eighty. Therefore, having had my fill of illness, bereavement and unhappiness, I escaped while I had the chance.

Although many times in the previous year I had felt that I would love to be picked up by some merciful, giant bluebird of happiness, carried away and dropped into a completely different life style, the idea of living anywhere other than England had never occurred to me. John and I had travelled around the world on many occasions but no matter how beautiful those far-away places had been, there was nowhere I wanted to live but at home and no one I wanted to be but me.

Yet now, being me, with this heavy heart and this head full of sadness, wasn't all that great any more. Worst of all, I wasn't needed – I was obsolete. For the past twenty years John had been my life and my work. Unlike many other women, I did not want a career. I loved my home, I was a domestic animal, and never were my talents more utilized than when John and Dad were ill.

It is a fact of life that, no matter how bad things become, somehow something is given to help us cope, a lesson learned, a new strength acquired. I found the ability to live in the present during that time, something I had never managed before when things were going well and the living was easy. Then my mind was constantly darting about, in the past or in the future, and now the future was too awful to contemplate. There was no room for drama; the reality of what was happening was drama enough and had to be turned into a casual everydayness. The next meal was about as far ahead as I could afford to think and John's or Dad's immediate needs were my only priority. In one way life became simpler because there were no choices to be made; there was only what was.

Dad's illness was a long and lingering affair. He developed cancer in his upper jaw, just under his left eye, and after an exploratory operation the doctors told me that it was hopeless, but that they would be able to prolong his life for a while with chemotherapy and deep ray treatment. The worst part for me was the period after the operation when I knew the truth and my parents did not, hearing them making plans for the future and saving my tears until I was alone. I wept more during that time than in the whole of the coming nightmare. By then I had become stronger.

As soon as Dad knew, things were easier. He had always been a brave man and this was his greatest test. Mother, the fatalist, wanted him to forgo the treatment and let the disease take its natural course, but Dad, ever the fighter, decided that he would prefer to have something tangible to wrestle with than sit in his armchair and wait for the end. I thank God he did because during that time I grew closer to him and found out more about him than ever before in my entire life.

The treatment was carried out at Canterbury hospital. For nearly a year I went with him to the outpatients every weekday. It was during this time that I found out so much more about my wonderful father and his extraordinary life. On the surface it was not exactly a pleasant way to pass the best part of nearly every day, waiting anything up to four hours in a draughty corridor among a queue of other cancer sufferers, but inside the situation wonderful things were given to me: the story of my father's life and his time, vividly told in the minutest detail, to the names of childhood friends, schoolteachers, snippets about my beloved grandmother, and Dad's life from the age of ten spent working alongside his father on the fishing trawlers. His ability to remember with such clarity amazed Dad every bit as much as it did me. His life was virtually passing before his eyes, and I was fortunate enough to be sitting next to him watching the same show.

During that time I learned the essence of the man, and I count myself lucky to have known him, and luckier still that he was my father. Sometimes – indeed, more often than not – being a parent or a child precludes the possibility of real, honest friendship, but the circumstances of his illness rewarded us both with unimagined riches.

After a year's remission, Dad began to decline in health once again. This time there was nothing to be done. His jaw was broken in several places as a result of the chemotherapy, he lost the sight of his left eye, and the cancer began to spread across his face causing a hideous disfigurement. What amazed everyone, even friends who saw him rarely, was the fact that, after the initial shock, we forgot his illness, such was the quality of his personality and the depth of his humour.

For all his suffering, he never complained; he was a man at peace with himself, well pleased with his life and prepared to meet the end of it. I bought him a tape recorder and made him record everything he had told me two years before. He was happy to do so; the past had reached out and embraced him and he was more there than anywhere. I was his prompt from the wings, keeping him to the point, guiding him through the stories I had already heard and which I knew to be too good to be lost with him. They are all filed carefully away, captured on tape for some time in the future when the sound of his voice, weakened by illness, may be less painful to bear.

We managed to get him into a hospice towards the end. I bless everyone who worked there. The day Mum and I took him in our hearts were very heavy, but we walked into a place of joy, where every patient was allowed to die with dignity, free of the pain which drives people crazy. I thank God that my father escaped that fate.

About two weeks before he died Dad wanted to come home, he knew that his end was near. One Sunday morning he began to bleed from the mouth. I called the hospice and they sent an ambulance.

'Don't worry, Dad, they're looking forward to seeing you,' I said.

'I'm not worried, old love,' he answered, as he held a towel to his face. 'I could do with a change.'

When the ambulance men arrived he said, 'Stop off at the Sportsman pub on the way.'

Not long after he was admitted he became delirious. He spent his last day as a child on the seafront at Ramsgate. His mother, my grandmother, was with him holding his hand through me.

'Look at the elephants, Mum,' he said excitedly. 'Blimey, what a parade, it looks like it's going on for ever.' And he chuckled with pleasure, his sightless old eyes watching the circus go past before he dropped into his last deep sleep.

From where I sit outside the cottage I can hear the voices of children on the beach muted and distant. It is a compelling sound; it never fails to draw me. It is the only time I feel a longing for something I have left behind – my granddaughter Emma. How she would love this day – this life – and how I should love to share it with her. The only thing I have brought with me from England is her photograph, because she is young, new, and full of present and future. Everything else is back there.

When I sold my house after Dad's death I moved back to Mother's and took over the top two floors of her house. What I couldn't get into my flat I packed into her huge cellar. I found myself unable to throw away a single thing, not a press cutting or a letter, a birthday card or a photograph, feeling that to do so would be an insult to John, like throwing away a piece of his life.

But here in Spain nothing of the past intrudes. Here is pristine newness and novelty. A sort of metamorphosis is going on and I quite like it. Here I am not John Le Mesurier's widow but 'the English lady who feeds the cats'. A friend who was visiting me lost her way and asked in a local shop if anyone knew an English woman who lived nearby. I was described as 'the English lady with the big tits'. And that is all I am here, a bit of a mystery, but someone who is accepted none the less.

I am constantly surprised at how little I miss all the modern conveniences of life, no washing machines or dishwashers to make life easier. No TV and video to distract and lull the senses. I have a small radio and tape machine, so I can play a bit of cheering Mozart or Vivaldi when the mood takes me. I have about six books: Austen, Trollope and Dickens, some of the writers I never seemed to find time for back in England and who are giving me great pleasure here. I sleep deeply in a narrow, hard little bed, and on waking the first thing that I see is a palm tree, underneath which five or six wild cats sit patiently waiting to be fed. It is very simple and pleasant having the cats as my only responsibility, and yet the days here seem to lack sufficient hours – I can't keep track of where they go to. There are none to be killed, that's for sure. After all, I have to fetch water every day as the tap water is salt. Then there's the firewood and the kindling to collect from the beach, the market to visit, the cats, who live on the rocks by the sea, to feed, and long precious hours of freedom in which to look, and look, and look.

I am looking inward a lot as well, finding out what I am like, what pleases me, and trying to indulge myself wherever possible. It is not difficult because all I really want is peace of mind and simplicity – no gourmet meals, smart clothes, grand hotels or boringly rich people. I am glutted on all that.

It is strange how my life seems to have come full circle lately. I feel as though I have come back to my roots. Living like a peasant comes naturally to me, so here in Spain I find it easy to look back beyond the events of the recent sad past, right back to the beginning of my life, and discover the similarities between then and now.

Two

Although I come from a loving, happy home, my very
first memory is of being whacked in the mouth by my
father – for what I have no idea, but I suspect it was for the
sin of poverty, overcrowding and the frustration which
dogged my father's footsteps throughout his early life. I
probably made one demand too many at the wrong
moment.

In my childhood there was nothing unusual about being
whacked – it was the normal way to put across a point to a
naughty child at home and at school – but how I burned
with the injustice of it. The answer to 'Why can't I?' was
always 'Because I say so!' and if – as was usually the case – I
requested further clarification, it was given in the form of a
stinging slap. Where it fell depended on how quickly I
dodged out of the way, but my head was usually the most
popular target. A good boxing of the ears probably sent
thousands of children reeling into adolescence half-cocked.

However, although my childhood was peppered by the
sound of slaps on one side, it was balanced on the other by
the smack of kisses, the benison of hugs and the sound of
laughter – most of the latter being supplied by Grandma
Long. She was my paternal grandmother, of Romany
blood, beautiful, dark-haired and willowy when young,
and by the time I came into her life still beautiful though
plump and curvy. Like a great soft cushion, Grandma and
her love padded the harsher edges of reality. She led me
through the years of the war, the brutality of school and
the injustice of poverty, blinkered and protected from
these things by her passion for fantasy, superstition, magic

and everything fey. Almost as soon as I could toddle I was led off to the Odeon cinema in Ramsgate where I quickly progressed from Shirley Temple to Bette Davis.

But to begin at the beginning. I was born in Oldham, Lancashire, in a private nursing home. Mother was always very proud of that fact. It was the only time in her life that she ever had anything private, so I have to give it a cursory mention. My father came from Ramsgate, Kent, which, in the days when he was a lad, was a popular holiday resort whose pride was its beautiful royal harbour and its fishing fleet. Grandpa Long was a skipper on a fishing trawler and he had worked his way up to this elevated position through a lifetime of slavery. He was brought up in an orphanage, then became a smack boy on a fishing boat where he started work at the age of ten. He never learned to read or write and had no idea where he came from. Mother, in her unkinder moments, used to say he had 'a touch of the tar brush' as he had a broad, pug nose, slanting eyes and high cheekbones. He was a lovely old man, a shadowy, benign figure in my early childhood.

During one of our sessions together at the end of his life, Dad told me that years before, Grandpa, who always liked a drink, had fallen off a ladder while climbing down to a trawler – he was pissed at the time – and had broken his leg. He cheerfully splinted it up himself and then went fishing for ten days. It had left him with a permanently bent leg, but he never complained. He had also, over the years, pulled every one of his own teeth out and had never gone to a doctor in his life. He was a tough old man whose presence caused scarcely a ripple in the daily routine of the house.

Dad, whose education ceased at the beginning of the First World War, joined him on the fishing boat at the age of twelve and, in spite of having no qualifications save a natural intelligence and an aptitude for hard work, was accepted by the Oldham Constabulary when he was twenty. In the course of his duty he was handed a stray dog one day by my pretty mother and soon after had the wit to marry her, thus embarking upon fifty-five years of love, fidelity and companionship. Mother was a mill girl, one of a large family, born and bred in Oldham, although her father, Grandpa Jones, was Welsh.

Dad had been in the police force for six years when he was injured while fighting a fire in a cotton mill. His left kneecap was shattered and he was invalided out of the service with a permanently damaged leg and a police pension. Mercifully the accident kept him out of active service when the war began. I remember nothing of this, being only one year old at the time, but for me it was a blessing in disguise because the accident prompted Dad to take Mother and me down to Ramsgate where I was claimed and doted upon by Grandma Long, and where my life really began.

Which brings me in a roundabout way back to my first memory, the smack in the mouth. I must have been about two at the time. We all lived at Grandma's, which was great for me, though not for Mother because she and Grandma didn't get on. Grandma's house wasn't clean enough by Mother's pristine standards, and they were as different as chalk and cheese, Mother being a practical, North Country, down-to-earth lass, and Grandma an emotional, generous peasant, giving hospitality to anyone who had a touching story.

We had two rooms at the top of the house where Mother tried her best to live a self-contained existence. There was a cooker on the landing and a sink in one of the rooms, which served as a kitchen cum dining room cum living room. There was but one bedroom, which must have interfered drastically with my parents' sex life, although I can't remember ever sleeping anywhere but with Grandma and Grandpa in a little bed in the corner of their room or living anywhere but downstairs, which, compared with the orderly gleaming neatness of Mother's domain, seemed to me like Aladdin's cave.

Grandma's territory was the semi-basement. It comprised a large kitchen with a big black cooking range where there was always something simmering. The kitchen was always warm and full of appetizing smells. In front of the range was a large rag rug which Grandma had made out of remnants of old clothing. She used to sit in her rocking chair with me on her soft ample lap and tell me stories about all the different materials, where they came from and whom they belonged to. Her tales were as colourful as the rug, woven together as they were into a magic carpet of fantasy.

'Grandma,' I'd say, pointing to a colourful piece of paisley, 'tell me about that one.'

'Ah, yes, now that's an interesting scrap – it was part of Raggity Jack's waistcoat. Now Jack was given to me one Christmas when I was about as old as you are . . .' and off she would go into a yarn, her eyes looking far away over my head into the past, while I bounced and rocked on her knee, devouring her tall tales hook, line and sinker.

In the big warm kitchen there was a long Welsh dresser cluttered with different coloured plates, bowls, dishes, cups and saucers, jugs, vases, ornaments and Grandpa's pipe cleaners. Anything that was lost usually came to light tucked somewhere on one of the shelves.

In the middle of the room was a large scrubbed table, where Grandma would chop her vegetables, roll her pastry, where I would do my crayoning and where the family would gather for meals. The table would change the whole mood of the room according to how it was dressed – bare and scrubbed for work, laid with a checkered tablecloth for everyday, a white damask one for Christmas and special occasions, and after meals a dark-green chenille one with a fringe. The kitchen led out to a garden, which was partly paved near the house and had an outside loo and a large iron clothes-wringer. There was also a zinc bath, which was brought into the house on Friday nights for the family to take turns in for their weekly submersion.

The garden, framed by high flint walls, was long and narrow, with flowerbeds on each side of a flagged path. It was Grandma's pride and passion. In the summer it was a blaze of colour, edged with scallop shells, blue lobelia, snapdragons, delphiniums and roses, and climbing up the old flint walls there was a profusion of wistaria. It was a picture in the summer and Grandma knew every stick and stalk of it. 'Look here,' she would say excitedly, pointing to a millimetre of something green which even my strong young eyes had trouble finding, 'that's a marigold to keep the greenflies away – there's another, and another.' And her keen gardener's eyes would pick out every new shoot to be nurtured into strong life under her loving care.

Last but not least was the front basement parlour. This was where my love of words and stories was born because it was here that Grandma and I listened to our afternoon radio plays. In the parlour there was a Victorian black iron fireplace, in front of which was another rag rug, two large armchairs and a black horsehair sofa. There was also a chiffonier and on this were some lustre vases and a collection of bric-à-brac, along with more of Grandpa's pipe cleaners.

Flanking the fireplace were two built-in cupboards to mantelpiece height, and on one of these, ear level to Grandma's chair, stood the radio – our little box of dreams. It was here, cuddled up on Grandma's lap, that I heard the story of Mary Rose, by J. M. Barrie, one winter's afternoon while the room darkened and the crackling fire cast shadows. With Mary Rose I was transported to the island where time stood still. Some of the plays were beyond my understanding, and then I would doze with my head on Grandma's enormous bosom, the comforting voices of the actors weaving into my dreams. After the play Grandma would leave me to doze on while she made the tea, which was always eaten in front of the fire in the parlour, and to this day the sound of cups clattering and the smell of toast gives me a pleasant feeling of security and comfort.

The highlight of the year was Christmas. Christmases at Grandma's have never been equalled. In my memories of her she always seems to be preparing for it; the cupboards in her bedroom were full of rustling secrets. The nights leading up to it were my favourite times, when the kitchen table was our workplace. I would sit at one end making chains out of rectangular pieces of gummed coloured paper, and at the other end Grandma prepared the coming feast, rolling out the pastry for the mince pies and sausage rolls, boiling a huge ham and preparing the stuffing for the turkey. Grandpa would go to the pub and bring back a big jug of beer for Grandma and a lemonade for me, and the two of us would sing carols while we worked away happily.

At bedtime I would climb the stairs behind her as she carried the oil lamp, holding on to her long black skirts in fear lest I, like Mary Rose, might be carried away. Grandpa, none too steady on his legs, would come behind, carrying the po.

After being unemployed for a few months after he first brought us to Ramsgate, Dad got a job at Merrie England, a huge amusement park on the seafront. Because of his experience in the Oldham Police he was employed as a commissionaire, a polite name for a bouncer. There were about six commissionaires working there altogether, all big, handsome men in smart brown uniforms trimmed with gold braid, and they kept law and order among the holidaymakers who flocked to Ramsgate during those carefree summers before the war.

In those days the amusement park was the mecca of all seaside towns, far more exciting than its equivalent today. For a start people were more gullible then, more willing to be taken in by the grafters who ran the darts stalls, the rifle ranges, the tombolas and the housey-housey (now called bingo) games, let alone by the brightly coloured façades of the side shows, where they were entertained by the silver-tongued spielers who gave them a sample of what to expect on the inside after they had parted with their silver sixpences.

Those were the days of beautiful roundabouts with

painted horses which carried you up into the air and down again while you hung on for dear life to the twisted pole in front of you. The calliope played selections from Gilbert and Sullivan as you began to move, slowly at first, and then faster and faster, until just before you got scared and thought you might fall off, the roundabout gradually slowed down, leaving you wanting more and begging not to be taken off.

But best of all for me were the freak shows. Dad would take me round to meet all the wonderful and unusual people, who spoiled me with sweets and games and magic tricks. They were all my friends. The gypsy fortune-teller would take me into her tent and give me biscuits and tell me stories about dead people. I would peer into her crystal ball, hoping to see wonderful pictures, but nothing but my own chubby, distorted little face would appear, though she assured me that one day I would be given the gift of second sight.

The snake charmers frightened me; they were Indians and fierce, and kept themselves to themselves. But the snakes were charming: they were full of mystery and glamour, slow-moving and beautiful. One day, while Grandma and I were watching hand in hand as the charmers were doing their front-of-house performance, a large rat ran out from under the stage into the crowd. Panic ensued. Quick as a flash one of the Indians leaped off the stage and came down hard right on the back of the poor creature, then proceeded to jump up and down on it until he had squashed it flat. I was led away in tears, all my sympathy going out to the animal which had met such an awful death.

The fat lady wore an outfit resembling baby-doll pyjamas in order to show off her acres of rubbery flesh, which she was always asking the crowd to pinch and touch. She wore pink ribbons in her hair and masses of make-up, and although she was always laughing, the sight of her depressed me.

My favourites were the midgets. They had their own

village, as it was called, in a corner of Merrie England, a huge walled area where they lived throughout the summer season, going about their daily lives oblivious of the crowds who stared down at them from a raised walkway which surrounded their domain. Sometimes Dad would drop me in among them and leave me to play, while Mum and Grandma went off for a drink or a cup of tea. It was wonderful to run around in my very own Munchkin land, playing at tea parties and games to my heart's content. They were kind, gentle people, all of them forced, in those poverty-plagued pre-war days, to cash in on their misfortunes and abnormalities in order to keep body and soul together. However, none of these problems were apparent to a privileged toddler like myself. To me it was all playtime, and what with Grandma and her stories, I never knew where reality left off and enchantment began.

Grandma loved Merrie England as much as I did. It was right up her street. She was especially fond of the oyster parlours. She could dispose of two dozen at a time, and although I didn't share her enthusiasm for the slimy delicacies, I watched in fascination as they disappeared down her throat in rapid succession while I ate a plate of peeled shrimps, and drank lemonade.

Our eating binges around Merrie England were the bane of Mother's life. Anything I fancied I was given: Ramsgate rock, chips, candyfloss, prawns. Then later, when I couldn't eat my tea or, as often happened, when I threw up during the night, Mother would go into a rage and curse Grandma to hell and back.

However, fate intervened and, as if to compensate her for Grandma's obsession with me, Mother gave birth to a boy. She called him David, and he was all hers. It also precipitated the need for my parents to find a place of their own, as Mother sure as hell wasn't going to have two of us under Grandma's spell.

The new house was about a quarter of a mile away, in an area with the attractive name of Dumpton Gap. Mother was thrilled; it was newly built and had a garden with a lawn. I wasn't too taken by it – it felt too cold and bare after the womb-like comfort of Grandma's – but it was everything that Mother had longed for ever since she arrived in Ramsgate. It turned out to be a fleeting luxury, however, because the rent of £1 a week proved to be beyond my father's means. The job at Merrie England brought in £2 10 shillings a week and was only seasonal. In the winter months it was a fight for survival, with Dad taking anything that came his way. He got a job as an insurance agent, no wages just commission, but it brought in lean pickings which didn't cover the rent. After a year we all trooped back to Grandma's, who fed and kept the lot of us for under £1.

This time Dad hit on the idea of selling dressed crabs from door to door. They were boiled up in a huge pan on Grandma's stove and the household reeled from the stench. The kitchen table, normally Grandma's sole territory, was Dad's workroom and tempers bubbled up with ever increasing frequency. Mother's role in all this was to go from door to door like a gypsy carrying the crabs in a huge basket. Every refusal was a personal rejection and her pride took a beating.

Nevertheless, in those days good honest work, whatever it was, earned respect, and Mother, unhappy though she might have been, worked alongside Dad uncomplainingly. Eventually a council house was allocated to them and once again we had a house with a garden where we rested for a few years. I began my schooling and Mother produced another baby, a boy called Terry.

When I was about six years old Dad got a job as the manager of the pier at Folkestone, another seaside town about twenty miles along the coast from Ramsgate. It was a step up in the world, as the pier was a popular tourist attraction, with an amusement park, skating rink, cafés, side shows and, at the far end, a dance hall where smart London bands played through the season.

Dad installed us in a nice flat in the centre of the town and exchanged his commissionaire's uniform for a smart white linen suit, while Mother took to wearing bell-bottom trousers and sleeveless blouses, had her eyebrows plucked and wore her hair in a marcel wave. They made a handsome couple and I suspect that it was the happiest time of their lives. They had a position: Dad was an employer – his staff called him Mr Long and looked up to him – while Mother was put in charge of the ballroom staff during the afternoon tea dances. Old photos reveal that she was indeed a glamorous sight and bore a striking resemblance to the film star Bebe Daniels, who was a current favourite in those days.

By then I had started school in Folkestone. Brother David was in kindergarten, and as Mother was now a career woman it was necessary to hire a nanny, a professional one from an agency, complete with starched white uniform and soul to match.

Mother was useless at handling staff. She had never done it before and on the day that Nanny Bridget arrived you could see from the very first moment who had the upper hand. We were all waiting in our best clothes in order to make an impression, and as soon as I looked into her eyes I knew with the intuition of the young that there was no kindness in her and that things were never going to be the same.

Nanny Bridget's first request was that she must have full control over us without interference. 'I'm a great believer in order and discipline, and I shall punish the children if it's necessary. But I'm sure that it won't come to that, will it, children?' she said, smiling at us, her eyes like ice. David and I nodded nervously, while Terry, too young to know the significance of this new presence in our midst, gurgled away in his playpen.

'The children may call me Bridget, unless you prefer that they call me Nanny,' she continued, 'and do you wish me to wear the uniform or my casual clothes?' Mother requested the mufti.

After showing her where everything was kept and how everything worked, Mother was dismissed, sent back to the pier. Bridget's first order was that I help her in tidying up every drawer and cupboard in the flat. 'I want to know where everything belongs, and I want you to know as well,' she said. 'And woe betide you if anything is not put in its rightful place in future.'

Woe certainly did betide me frequently after that. The first shock was at lunchtime. After we had washed our hands and faces to her meticulous satisfaction, we sat down at table. 'Now, clasp your hands together, bow your heads, and repeat after me "For what we are about to receive may the Lord make us truly grateful."' We had never heard of grace and what was presented to us made us anything but grateful. Boiled potatoes, overcooked cabbage and large, rubbery lumps of fat, with hardly a scrap of lean meat clinging to them. 'I want every morsel of food to be chewed and your plates cleared, or woe betide you,' said Bridget menacingly.

'I can't eat the fat,' I said in disbelief.

'Can't? What is this word "can't"?'

My little brother, not yet four years old, began to cry. 'I want my mummy, I'm not hungry.'

This was right up Bridget's street. 'Naughty, disobedient children are not allowed to see their mummies and daddies until Nanny has turned them into good, obedient ones. You are both forbidden to go near the pier unless I take you, and I'll take you there only when you deserve it and do as you are told. *I* am telling you to eat up every morsel of food on your plates, and while you chew, I want you to think hard about all the hungry children in the world and to thank the Lord for all your blessings.'

There was nothing to be done but obey. In went the yellow cubes of fat one by one. My gorge rose as I chewed. I quickly learned to pretend to chew and to force the lumps down whole – the underdone potatoes and watery cabbage were like manna from heaven by comparison – and I gradually heaved and swallowed my way through what was to be the first of hundreds of nightmare meals.

My sensitive little brother fared far worse than I. He

sobbed and chewed as best he could, but he was a faddy child at the best of times, with a small appetite, and it was all too much for him.

'Very well,' said our tormentor, 'if we don't finish our dinner we get no pudding. And so as not to see what the rest of us are eating, we go and stand in the corner and think about all the hungry little children.'

For the first time in my life I learned the meaning of hate and fear. I forced down my puddingy reward while David stood in the corner shaking with sobs.

A little later, after he had stood there for an hour while I helped Bridget clear the table and tidy up, we were taken for a walk. Terry was in his pram, and David and I had to walk along on either side with instructions to hold on to it. It was early spring of our second year in Folkestone. The pier was open for the tea dances and the fishermen, as it had been all winter, but now the preparations for the coming season were in full swing. The stalls were painted and the roundabouts unwrapped from their canvas winter overcoats. Although it was still cold, the promise of summer beckoned all around us. The Leas Cliffs were rustling with life, the bracken was unfurling and the daffies were making way for the wallflowers and sweet betsy. Below lay the pier, and Mum and Dad.

Just wait till I tell them how you treat us, Bridget, I thought as I walked obediently along the clifftop holding on to the pram as I had been ordered. Just you wait.

As it happened, I was the one who had to do the waiting as we weren't taken to the pier on that day or any other. By the time Mum and Dad came home from work in the evenings we were all fast asleep, and in the mornings I was off to school and David to kindergarten. Terry was too young to understand the physical and mental cruelty that was being inflicted on us. It was a week before we even set eyes on our parents and by that time we were in deathly fear of Bridget. It wasn't that she beat us very often – she was too clever for that; it was more her relentless discipline and the humiliation of her punishments, the humiliation of being shown up in front of each other, of being made to stand in the corner for weeping at mealtimes, and eventually of our pathetic attempts to ingratiate ourselves with her for the reward of one of her smug, triumphant smiles and the relief of being let off an extra piece of fat.

Mother had given Bridget an allowance on which to run the house and feed us, but as she was seldom at home she had no idea what sort of food we were being given. Bridget must have made quite a bit of pin money out of the housekeeping. When we were presented to them for approval under Bridget's hawklike supervision, my parents saw only two beautifully behaved model children.

In those mutton-fat-plagued days of the summer of 1939 things were happening across the Channel that were going drastically to change our lives, but all we knew was the dread of mealtimes, the longing for kindness and the fear of punishment.

One Saturday, when we were by ourselves on the pebble beach playing tightrope walkers on one of the great iron pipes which ran out to sea, I fell off and hit my head. An egg-sized lump appeared and I was in so much pain that I threw caution to the winds and, with David in tow, ran screaming to the pier to find Mum and Dad. While we were being fussed and pampered by Mother and the kindly waitress from the ballroom, we told Mother about Bridget and what she did to us, what she made us eat. We begged Mother not to let her know we had been near the pier. On this occasion Mother obviously chose not be believe us.

On the following Monday I arrived home from school to find David standing trouserless and crying in the corner, his poor bum red and sore from a beating he had received for denying that we had been to the pier the previous Saturday. He had wet himself with fear under Bridget's interrogation and was punished doubly hard, once for lying and once for being a dirty little boy. When I saw this pathetic sight I ran to cuddle and protect him, admitting that we had indeed been to the pier. I was commended for my honesty and then punished for the double sin of disobeying Bridget by going to the pier and for refusing her order to leave a 'naughty little boy' to his punishment. David spent the rest of the day in bed and we were never allowed to go to the beach unaccompanied again.

The summer dragged on. All joy was missing from those sunlit days, but gradually Mother was beginning to suspect that things were not as they appeared on the surface. For one thing, David had developed a stammer. He already had a lisp. I could understand him and was his translator but Bridget, in trying to get him to speak clearly, had bullied him to such an extent that he became afraid to speak at all.

The crunch came, however, when, on returning from school one day, I found my brother Terry, who was only about nineteen months old, standing on a chair at the kitchen sink trying to wash his pants. He was sobbing uncontrollably, David was cowering in a corner, and Bridget, her face red with rage, was yelling, 'I'll get you clean if it's the last thing I do, you disgusting little devil.'

She had been trying to potty-train him, had taken his nappy off, and when he had dirtied himself she had flown into a rage and beaten him. Then she had made him stand on the chair at the sink and wash his pants.

It was the last straw as far as I was concerned. I took in the scene and my suppressed hatred overflowed. 'Leave him alone!' I screamed, and rushed to rescue my brother. 'You rotten bully!'

Her eyes popping in disbelief, Bridget rounded on me. 'Get upstairs at once and stay in your room. I'll deal with you later,' she shouted.

But I was too quick for her. 'I'm going to get my father. I'm going to tell him what you've done.' And I ducked out of the way of her swinging slap and rushed from the flat, sobbing with rage.

I ran all the way to the pier, fear giving wings to my feet, and collapsed around my mother's waist, gasping out my story, pleading with her to do something. And this time she took notice. I was left on the pier to be comforted by the waitress again, while Mum and Dad hurried to the flat. I don't know what transpired between them and Bridget, but the next day Bridget departed, leaving behind nothing but a hated memory and a loathing for fatty meat which remains with David and me to this day.

After Bridget came Elsie, not from an agency this time, but from the snack bar on the pier. A thin, chirpy Cockney sparrow, she was entirely different from Bridget. Mother told me years later that in fact she was sloppy, dirty and none too reliable, but to us children she was a saint. She may have left fat splashes round the cooker, but she spent her time with us bestowing the love and happiness that Bridget had denied us for so long. Mealtimes became a pleasure once more – melted cheese on toast, boiled eggs for tea, and chips with everything. There was noise and laughter around the table instead of silence and dread. David developed a passion for her and she for him. He had been damaged more than Terry and I by Bridget's sadistic discipline, and although his stammer was to be a legacy that took years to cure, his heart was soon mended by Elsie's loving care.

One fine sunny afternoon in September we were on the pier with Elsie when the sirens announced the outbreak of the Second World War. Elsie hurried us off to find our parents and I knew by her fear that this was something very serious.

'It's an air-raid, Mr Long,' said Elsie. 'We're going to be bombed.'

'What's an air-raid? What's bombed?' I asked, frightened. These were new words to me and I didn't like the sound of them at all.

'Come on, Elsie, don't frighten the kids,' said Dad. 'Nothing's going to happen this early.'

But big changes were coming. The first one filled me with joy: I was to go back to Ramsgate to stay with Grandma while my parents made reluctant preparations to move back to Oldham.

Back at Grandma's all was as solid and as comforting as

usual, only better because, now that I was older and with the uncertainty surrounding the future, Grandma escaped more and more from reality by taking me to the pictures almost every afternoon. As the cinemas changed their programmes twice weekly, and there were three of them in Ramsgate, we covered a lot of ground. Bette Davis was our undisputed favourite. I'll never forget the rush of pleasure as the lights dimmed and the gittering phoney world of make-believe swept us both away. Grandma's lap was always loaded with a selection of sweets and she had a large handkerchief at the ready as she could be awash with tears one minute and shaking with laughter the next. The newsreel pictures of the soldiers going off to war had her sobbing uncontrollably, and I would pat her hand in an attempt to console her, still unmindful of the horror of what was happening, aware only of the excitement of this new turn of events.

At the beginning of the autumn term I started a new school. I had a natural aptitude for reading which had been encouraged at Folkestone, and I was way ahead of the other children in my class. While the rest of them were struggling through junior readers, I had progressed to Tom and the Waterbabies and A. A. Milne. I was often made to read aloud to the class, which I loved, being a bit of a show-off. Then the air-raids began.

Ramsgate had the advantage of hundreds of underground tunnels, many of which had been used by smugglers in the days when contraband was the town's main source of revenue. When the war began the tunnels were brought back into service as air-raid shelters and entrances to them were dug out at strategic places. One of these was at the bottom of our hill, and there was another at the top. As we lived halfway up we had two options for survival. The one at the bottom was our first choice as it led straight into the main tunnel and was deeper underground.

The shelling began first, and then came the incendiary bombs. Being near Manston Airport, Ramsgate was a prime target and also a dumping ground for the bombers which had not managed to reach London.

Grandma, though terrified when the bombing got under way, rose to the challenge. She bought me a siren suit, a sort of padded boiler suit, which she made me sleep in, so that at the first note of the air-raid warning we could be out of bed in a flash and off down the hill. Every night she packed her old oilcloth bag with a Thermos flask and food in readiness, and although she was a big woman, the speed with which she rushed me down the hill was nothing short of mercurial.

Grandpa, after one or two visits to the tunnels, decided that he would prefer to take his chances and stay in his own bed. All Grandma's pleading was in vain. But for me the whole thing was a great adventure. My friends and I longed for clear moonlit nights. They were the nights when the bombers came and a night in the tunnels meant games and sing-songs.

Eventually we were all allocated our own niches. Of course, Grandma's was the most comfortable, with a bunk bed, a stove and a chair or two. Lino-covered orange boxes were converted into shelves, coconut matting covered the chalk floor and the recess was curtained off for privacy. There was no privacy from the night noises, however. Snores of every description whistled through the tunnels, the murmur of voices muffled in anger or hushed in love. The odd fart would ring out.

'Christ, that one was close,' someone would comment.

'Yeah, by the smell, I think it got the gasworks,' some wit would reply.

The feeling of camaraderie was everywhere. We were all united against a common foe; cheerfulness and good humour prevailed under the most trying and primitive conditions. Possessions lost their importance: houses full of treasured mementos could be blown away in a minute, and when a family emerged from the tunnels after a raid to find that they had been bombed out, everyone rallied round and shared what they had with their less fortunate neighbours. Life was all that mattered, and the prospect of victory over the hated Hun.

Eventually, as the shelling worsened, the whole town moved permanently underground and the population became a race of troglodytes. I didn't care as long as I had Grandma to cuddle up to in the tunnel at night while she romanced away, taking my mind far from things as they were to things as she would like them to be. School closed down, home became a place where we went to have a quick wash and a change of clothes, personal hygiene became harder to maintain even though water and chemical lavatories had been laid on underground. Nevertheless, a shampoo was a luxury, let alone a bath. To us children running wild through the labyrinthine maze of chalk streets it was an added treat not to have to wash regularly or clean our teeth twice a day, but, alas, only a temporary one. One day Dad, bereft now of his smart white suit which, along with his job, had gone for good, came to get me. Grandma, awash with tears, packed my few possessions and handed me over, vowing that she would join us all in Oldham if the war continued for much longer.

Back in Folkestone it was hard to believe the changes that had taken place in such a short space of time. The flat was stacked with packing cases, the walls were bare of pictures and only the basic utensils for cooking and cleaning were in evidence. Mother looked haggard and depressed, and the sight of me did little to cheer her up.

'You're filthy,' she exclaimed in horror. 'Get your clothes off right away and let me clean you up.' And she muttered and grumbled her way through the delousing which followed. It seemed that I had nits, which was only to be expected under the circumstances, and my clothes were none too clean, but it was very unfair to blame Grandma. She had done her best, and to hear her being accused of slovenliness and sloth after all the effort she had put into trying to make some sort of home for us under the most trying conditions brought tears to my

27

eyes already stinging from Derbac soap and carbolic.

Poor Mother, throughout the years of my childhood she was always overshadowed by my grandmother. I can understand her frustration now, but then I resented it. Perhaps because I was the object of so much affection from Grandma Mother felt it unnecessary to waste any more on me. Perhaps it was jealousy. I don't know, but it seemed that any slaps going were given to me rather than to my brothers. What angered me most was never being allowed to plead my cause – a slap in the mouth ended any arguments. It made me angry at the injustice of it all, especially as I could never remember a time when Grandma resorted to violence. Mother was up against hard competition. She was no worse than any other harassed young mother faced with poverty, three children, and the horror and uncertainty that were all around us in the early days of the war. To make matters worse, Dad had been drafted for work as a fire warden at Dover harbour, and as it was essential war work he couldn't join us in Oldham until he had obtained a transfer to a munitions factory. It could have been worse – without his disability he might have been drafted into the armed forces – but it was bad enough for poor Mother. She had been given one wonderful year when everything seemed to be going her way, one year of glamour, marcel waves, manicures and smart clothes, tea dances, admiration and flattery, and here she was delousing a dirty, sullen little girl in a bare flat surrounded by packing cases in preparation to flee to an uncertain future in Oldham. No wonder she was short-tempered.

A few days later we bade a tearful goodbye to my father at Folkestone station. Mother was looking careworn, Dad was trying to reassure her that he would be in Oldham before she knew it, the two boys were excited and fidgety, and I was still resentful at being snatched away from Grandma. I knew full well from Mother's tears that the future didn't hold much to be happy about. The journey north is a blur in my memory: all I can remember is that the train was crowded, we were bored and irritable, and Mother wept a lot.

The station in Manchester did little to dispel my inner foreboding, but at least Grandpa Jones and jolly Uncle Billy were waiting for us. They had hired a Daimler to take us all to Chadderton, a suburb of Oldham where Mother's family lived. But how my small heart dropped on the way to Grandma Jones's house as I peered out of the window at row upon row of dark, ugly streets.

The house was a Victorian grey stone terrace next to the police station and within spitting distance of Mother's entire family, most of whom I had never seen before. They were all well meaning and kind, but to me they all seemed like foreigners with their strange accents and mannerisms. The house was strange too. It smelt different and was more austere than Grandma Long's. She had gas lights and oil lamps, and here was bright overhead electric light, which made the place look cold and unwelcoming. What was worse, David and I couldn't even sleep there, as there was only room for Mother and baby Terry. We had to go and stay with jolly Uncle Billy and his wife, Auntie Jean, who wasn't at all jolly, probably because their marriage was on the rocks due to the fact that Uncle Billy was a bit too jolly, but not with Auntie Jean.

So, after a meal of muffins and tripe, which we kids couldn't eat because it reminded us of Bridget's loathsome mutton-fat cubes, we were led away weeping with exhaustion and bedded down on a makeshift bed on the floor in a strange house in a strange town among strangers.

Much of what happened during the settling-in weeks has faded from memory. It wasn't all bad, but in retrospect it seems as if the Oldham years were illuminated by a light of a dimmer wattage than before. Children quickly absorb change, and we grew accustomed to the clatter of clogs on the cobblestones in the early morning as the factory workers went off to the cotton mills which stood above the town like ugly black gravestones.

We became used to the strange food and the water closet

in the yard at the back of Grandma Jones's house. To use it we had to climb on to a high wooden platform with a step up and a long drop below, where the weight of excrement eventually tilted the disc at the bottom so it was deposited into the sewer. The whole contraption fascinated and frightened my brother and me. Grandma told us a horror story about a kitten which had been put down a water closet such as ours. It gave me nightmares and having nightmares at Auntie Jean's was doubly horrendous, because she certainly wasn't about to give out any motherly comfort in the small hours of the morning and jolly Uncle Billy was anything but jolly behind his own front door.

At Grandma Jones's things were decidedly better. Most evenings after tea Auntie Dorothy would play the piano and the whole family, being of Welsh descent, would always gather round and have a sing-song. This sort of thing was right up my street and I raised my voice to the rafters. I quickly learned the words to all the hit songs of the day – 'Romona', 'In a Little Spanish Town', 'Charmaine' – and later on all the Second World War songs – 'Silver Wings in the Moonlight', 'My Lovely Russian Rose', 'Room 504'. I can remember the words to this day.

The other good thing about Grandma Jones's house was Grandpa's front parlour. It was a grim, cold room full of heavy furniture, including a large Victorian bookcase with a glass front which contained Grandpa's collection of the complete works of Dickens and Auntie Dorothy's schoolgirls' annuals. Between those pages a world was revealed to me that I was only to glimpse in my dreams, the world of the boarding school where beautiful young girls who had mumsies and paters lived at places called 'The Grange' during the hols and were always doing brave things for the honour of Greystones or St Benet's. This was where my heart lay, the stuff of my daydreams, and from then on I escaped. At every conceivable opportunity I was to be found sitting on the black horsehair sofa miles away from Lowry land, somewhere on the playing fields of academe, calling out, 'Oh, well played, Bunty,' while my head-girl badge glinted in the sunshine.

The awful reality was just about as far from the dream as it was possible to be. Reality was a small soot-blackened torture chamber called St Mark's. It consisted of three classrooms and a small schoolyard surrounded by a high brick wall, which seemed to have permanently trapped the unhappiness and fear of thousands of children during the many decades of its existence. Because of the war it had been necessary to recall from retirement many teachers. The one who lay in wait for me was an evil old monster called by some ill-fated coincidence – Miss Bridget.

The second Miss Bridget bore a striking resemblance to Queen Victoria and was certainly never amused, unless she was breaking the spirit of some poor underprivileged child. Across the top of her high desk she kept her cane, a large thick piece of bamboo, which she used with relish and regularity. A spelling mistake or a fidget merited one stroke on the hand. For dirty work or nasty habits, such as picking the nose or scratching, we were given one stroke on each hand. For impertinence or giggling – well, if anyone was daft enough to give her some cheek or to find anything to laugh about – he or she got two behind the knees.

On my first day I was taken by Mother ostensibly to see how I liked it, not knowing that arrangements had already been made for me to start then and there. On entering the classroom the picture before me closely resembled one of the illustrations from Grandma's works of Charles Dickens – cowed, ragged children with clogs on their feet, high windows to prevent any views that might distract the mind and, sitting up high in front like a fat black crow, Miss Bridget peering over her steel-rimmed glasses at her latest victim. It was all so far removed from my dreams of Bunty of the Upper Fifth that I thought I'd gone back in time and I tried to beat a hasty retreat. A pitiful scene ensued with Mother trying to disentangle me from around her waist in front of the whole class, while Miss Bridget, who had terrorized Mother in her childhood, looked on with an anticipatory gleam in her eye. From then on I was marked for special treatment. I was the foreigner, my speech was different – according to Mother we spoke rather well – I was also 'the cowardly little girl who didn't like school', and I was going to be brought into line with the others.

I spent three years under the shadow of Miss Bridget's tender care. The main object of her method of teaching was to smother any spark of self-esteem, individuality or joy in a child. One event in particular illustrates her callousness. We were visited periodically by a district nurse, whose presence in the classroom would cause bowel-melting fear and consternation because, in the event of an infestation of nits, the victim's name was called out in front of the whole class, giving the poor child the status of pariah. Later the victim's hair was shaved off.

The ragged, shy little girl who sat at the same double desk as me came from an area of Chadderton called Old Busk which was known to be at the very bottom of the slum area. She was called Brenda Dobbs, and even though she sat next to me I can't remember ever hearing her speak. Poor Brenda's head had been shaved, adding to her feeling of inferiority, and her head was covered by a knitted dark green pixiehood.

One morning, as Miss Bridget paced up and down the aisles, she stopped at our desk – this was always a heart-lurching moment – and, looking down at poor Brenda, she snatched the pixiehood off her head. 'Don't wear that thing in class, child' she said. 'Your hair will never grow back.' Brenda, her bald, stubbly head revealed to the whole class, who showed their sympathy by a chorus of muffled giggles, sat trembling so violently with shame that waves of it seemed to enter into me. I sat paralysed with shock as, unable to control herself, she peed, soaking my gymslip and clogs in the process, until Miss Bridget hauled us out to the cloakroom to clean ourselves up.

I remember nothing more of that incident. The girl

stayed on, her hair grew back; whether or not the unseen scars ever healed I shall never know. Her parents, if she had any, never came to the school to knock the living shit out of Miss Bridget, as one would have hoped, and the reign of terror continued.

To our great joy, Dad eventually joined us and we moved at last to a home of our own. It was a dump of a place on Middleton Road, Chadderton, just a few minutes from Grandma and Grandpa Jones's. It was behind and over an empty shop, which with its large oak counters and shelf-lined walls, was a marvellous place for us children to play in. Dad did his best to fix up the rest of the place, which had no beauty whatever. But there was one advantage, one redeeming feature about it which made everything worthwhile.

We had a yard, long, narrow and ugly, with a back gate that opened on to an alleyway. And directly opposite our gate was the exit door of the Lyric cinema, the local fleapit, the passport to bliss, the house of pleasure which made a dishonest woman out of me. The price of admission to the first two rows was twopence, a sum not greatly missed from Mum's purse or Dad's trouser pocket. Every available opportunity would find me in the front two rows, peering up with neckbreaking devotion at the distorted faces of my idols. Sometimes, when twopence couldn't be obtained by theft or begging, I risked all by bunking in through the back door, if it was left open long enough for me, ever on the alert, to seize the opportunity for another glimpse of Don Ameche or Fred Astaire in Rio or Argentina or anywhere other than Chadderton, Oldham, in those dismal days. On summer evenings, when the projection room door was open, I could always be found sitting on top of the asphalt-roofed shed listening to the soundtrack. I knew every word of every film to find its way to the Lyric during those years and that's how I got by, muffled in dreams.

Of course, my schooling suffered. How could I be expected to master the intricacies of arithmetic and the dates of historical happenings when Carmen Miranda was prancing about at the Lyric. The welts on my hands became so bad that at times it was painful supporting the huge volume of Dickens in Grandpa's parlour.

The months passed and gradually I acquired a few friends. One was Betty Connolly, who lived in a street nearby in a house that smelled of pee. Her mother always seemed to be either shouting or putting on her make-up in front of the mirror over the fireplace prior to going out with one or other of Betty's 'uncles'. I remember Betty particularly well because she shared my fantasies. Betty was almost always house-bound, baby-sitting for her younger brothers and sisters – the source of the urine smell – and she was my alibi when I was at the pictures enjoying my stolen twopenn'orth of bliss. Betty and I would sit on her front step on summer evenings listening out for the children, describing the dresses we would wear when Messrs Gable or Ameche took us dancing on starry nights in Havana. Trapped by poverty and war in that awful little town, our feet were literally in the gutter but our heads were in the stars.

I had another friend, another social outcast because she was deaf and dumb, as was her whole family, some of whom were deaf, dumb and blind. She was called Mary and she lived a few doors away from us in Middleton Road. Her parents were Mormons, and they used to take me to their socials, which were held weekly in a little church hall with a corrugated-iron roof. I loved these evenings. There was always hymn singing, which I enjoyed, and we ended the evenings with bowls of black peas covered with vinegar, salt and pepper which made me fart all the way home, the sound mercifully unnoticed by the poor deaf and dumb family.

Mary taught me sign language and soon I was able to talk by touch to her poor old grandmother, who was totally afflicted. The family was so kind and gentle that, more to please them than anything else, I was baptized a Mormon. I signed the temperance pledge and vowed that I would make my way to Salt Lake City at the earliest possible opportunity. To my shame I lost interest in the whole thing when the family eventually moved away.

The gap she left was filled soon after by my beloved grandparents from Ramsgate, driven at last from their home by the war games being played directly above them. Dad and I went to Manchester to meet them. I was sick with excitement at the thought of having Grandma's company again. She was standing there in tears, a latter-day Ruth amid the alien mills. It can't have been easy for Mum to take them in or for Grandma to adjust to another person's home. There were the odd spats and sulks. But the war years brought out the best in everyone and they soldiered on, united by a common enemy. For me it was pure joy having Grandma there. She taught me to knit and, eager to do our bit, we made balaclava helmets and fingerless gloves for our fighting boys while listening to the radio in companionable silence. And there was the Lyric cinema. Grandma saving me from a life of crime by taking me with her at every possible opportunity.

And so we all lumbered through the dreary years of war. Grandma got a job in a wool shop owned by her brother who had lived in Oldham ever since he had gone there with Dad to join the police force all those years before. Uncle Harry had got a market concession, and I would go with Grandma to work on the wool stall at Tommy Field every weekend, showing an aptitude for sums that escaped me when sitting under the shadow of Miss Bridget's cane.

At eleven years of age I passed dizzy with relief from under her baleful eye to Eustace Street School in Chadderton. The school was large enough to get lost in and there was only one exponent of the Marquis de Sade method of teaching. I wasn't there long enough to have the nervous breakdown that she strove so hard to bring about in her pupils because something wonderful happened.

Dad managed to get a fairground concession on the Golden Mile in Blackpool and, in the space of a few hectic weeks, we were off to begin another phase of our lives. I left with hardly a backward glance, my only regret being that Grandma and Grandpa Long didn't come with us. They had settled down into a routine of sorts in the Middleton Road house, and Grandma said that the next move she would make would be the one that took her back to Ramsgate.

So, after bidding her a tearful goodbye, off I went, away from the mills and the memories, to spend the remaining years of the war in the sinful city of Blackpool.

Three

During the second half of the war Blackpool was a boom town. Its sole purpose was to offer pleasure and escape to the warweary, who flocked there to spend their holidays and money. It was a melting pot of different nationalities: Poles, Free French and Americans from the air bases nearby, heroes with fat bottoms and wallets to match swaggering through the town, their accents straight out of the movies proclaiming by their patronizing attitude and their glamorous uniforms that they had arrived in the nick of time to get 'little ol' England' out of trouble. There was money to burn and Blackpool was the bonfire, a northern Sodom and Gomorrah offering its tawdry pleasures to a public ready and willing to be charmed and conned into forgetfulness. It was a mecca for prostitutes, who arrived from all over England to clean up and at night they and their clients could be seen humping away in rows. Everyone happily engaged in one glorious communal orgasm.

Dad had a job running the children's playground near Central Station, and at weekends, in a little kiosk, I worked selling tickets for the swings, rides and roundabouts, and changing records of pop music which was relayed through a loudspeaker. I was as happy as a beaver to be part of the crazy glittering show.

Dad also had shares in an amusement arcade called the Happydrome, which had a snack bar, pinball machines, a bingo stall and, at the back, a freak show. The one I remember most vividly was Zsa Zsa, the Tattooed Bride. At the front of the arcade was an enormous hoarding displaying a painting of a glamorous pin-up in a bikini and covered in tattoos. Dad, every inch the showman, would stand on a platform and entice the sex-starved members of the armed forces and holidaymaking munitions workers to pay for a lascivious glimpse of the provocative creature inside, who was 'eager to reveal her secret charms'. Unfortunately in the flesh Zsa Zsa was a bitter disappointment. She was actually in her sixties. Fat and forbidding, she wore spectacles, was incredibly plain and had no personality whatsoever. She would stand in a pit, wearing a two-piece bathing suit and, with the aid of a cane, point out in a monotonous northern accent the amazing array of paisley-like images which covered her shapeless body while the male punters surveyed her in dismayed disbelief.

I took her and the other visiting 'freaks' in my stride at the time, feeling no curiosity whatever as to how she came to be so arrayed. It turned out that she was deeply religious and when she wasn't working was a Sunday-school teacher, her thick lisle stockings and sensible clothes hiding her fascinating secrets from the world.

The school that was found for me was called Tyldesley. A girls' school, it was famous for its choir, had a marvellous music teacher and, after St Mark's and Eustace Street, seemed like Utopia. There was an enormous gym, with wall bars, ropes, a window ladder and a shower room where, after our physical training sessions, we all stripped to the buff together. It was embarrassing at first, but wonderful fun when I lost my shyness. To my amazement, the teachers were all human beings, not a cane among them. I simply couldn't believe my luck, I fell in love with my English teacher Miss Wells, who was amazed at my knowledge of the works of Charles Dickens and my greed for literature of all kinds. She took me under her wing and bred in me a love of poetry, for which I bless her memory.

My life has been full of extremes, like a roller coaster. Even at this late stage I can't be sure if I've done these things to my life or if life has done them to me. I like to think that life has dealt me the cards and that everything given and taken has been for a great karmic reason which will only be made clear when I fall off my perch. It's a much more comforting theory now that I am older and it enables me to sit back and see what happens, instead of running up all those blind alleys, as I did in those early days during the war. But youth was born to run, and in my youth I never seemed to stop, especially after I hit Blackpool.

As the years passed my work on the Golden Mile increased. I was a Jack-of-all-trades, dashing from the playground to sell tickets on the bingo stall, help make tea and sandwiches in the snack bar, and even run a stall which Dad had set up at the back entrance of the children's playground, past which the new arrivals had to pass on their way from Central Station.

This stall was a gold mine. It consisted of two orange boxes, with a couple of planks covered in lino across the top. All we sold was cheap Indian perfume, perspex combs and knicker elastic, the latter being impossible to find in any large quantities. As *directoires* were still worn, not to mention gym knickers, it was a valuable commodity. I'm ashamed to admit that Dad, along with the rest of his colleagues, bought most of his gear on the black market during the war. Anybody who had the cash could buy just about anything and Dad knew a few Americans who worked in the kitchen on the nearby base. Suddenly wonderful things began to appear at home: sweets, American processed cheese, cookies and eggs – bowls of them. Our wartime pallor was replaced by the glow that comes from a good intake of protein, and life, though hectic, was full and happy. No time for dreams now, reality was far too exciting.

We had a flat right in the middle of Blackpool. It was over a shop in Chapel Street, which was in a direct line with Central Pier and round the corner from the Golden Mile. At the back of our street was an alleyway where the prostitutes who couldn't get a space under the pier took their customers for a knee-trembler. Naturally David and I in our innocence didn't know what they were doing. We didn't even know that prostitutes existed, for that matter. We just thought that people were very much in love in those days and did a lot of kissing. From time to time, though, there would be a fracas in the alley with shrill voices raised in anger after some poor working girl hadn't been paid for providing her services.

It was Sin City all right. On one occasion, as I was talking to some of my schoolgirl friends in Chapel Street, a great slob of an American came up to us. 'Any of you girls want to earn yourselves a pound?' he asked. Even though we didn't know what he wanted us to do, we knew that it was something 'not very nice'. The most common finds on Blackpool sands in those days were used french letters and sanitary towels. But it was still wonderful to have a beach to play on, even if the seaside donkeys did have to pick their way through old condoms.

During my thirteenth year I got a job working for a friend of Dad's on Central Pier. Bert was an old music hall artist, and he and his wife Doris had been a mind-reading act. They had gone into retirement some years before, but the rich pickings in Blackpool had been too fruitful to resist, so they had invented a mind-reading robot called Willy, the Amazing Talking Robot. Willy not only answered questions but printed your fortune by picking up your vibrations and transferring them on to paper by means of a printing press concealed in its back. This was visible through a glass panel so that the gullible punters could see the machine doing its extraordinary magic.

My job was to sit on a stool next to Willy, plunge my hand through a flap in his side, wave the fortunes (still wet from the press) to dry it, and relieve the poor suckers of a shilling, while Doris, concealed in a hut nearby, answered the questions put to her by Bert through a microphone which distorted her voice. Eventually I learned the code, and when Doris wanted a break I was allowed to be her stand-in. I was in show business.

When I was fourteen I left school, to my deep regret. I

had acquired a thirst for knowledge and would have liked to go on. But I was needed on the Golden Mile. I enrolled for evening classes, but during the summer months it was impossible for me to attend them. I loved my father deeply and the colourful life that I shared with him. But how I regretted being deprived of an education. Mine was so meagre that even now I feel a sense of inadequacy which certainly held me back when I tried to get a decent job earlier in my life.

During what was to be our last year in Blackpool Grandma came to visit a few times. She liked Blackpool well enough, but being by the seaside made her even more homesick for Ramsgate. She talked incessantly about it and made plans about our first Christmas there when the war ended.

Our place in Middleton Road had been filled by Dad's brother Harry, his wife May and their son Donald, like us, refugees from Ramsgate. One day Auntie May sent for Mum. She was worried about Grandma, who had had bronchitis, and wasn't picking up very well. May was worried about Grandma's state of mind as she was deeply depressed.

Dad couldn't leave work; he thought she just needed cheering up, and so Mum went alone. Grandma was in bed and her first words on seeing Mum were, 'I'm going home soon, Nell. It's nearly over (meaning the war), and I don't belong here.' She held tightly to Mum's hand, the tears streaming down her face, her great old body shaking with sobs. Mother consoled her as best she could and stayed with her until she slept. If there had been love lost between them in the past, I like to think that it was found in that short moment together, because later that afternoon when Mother looked in on her Grandma was dead. Her homesick soul, unable to wait any longer, had gone on ahead, back to her beloved Ramsgate.

I was inconsolable. That there was no Grandma in the world just wasn't possible. She was my best friend, my support. Her love for me had been the only true certainty in my life. Her company a never-wavering joy. Of course I knew that Mum and Dad loved me, but at times, as in all families, there were rows and harsh words. Never from Grandma, only praise and approval. The truth is, I was spoilt by her and I needed to be spoiled. How could I go through life without it? In my grief it never occurred to me that anyone else would miss her too, Grandpa, for instance. She was mine, a part of me, and I wailed like a banshee for God to give her back. But she was gone, leaving nothing except an unfinished piece of knitting and a great big hole in the world.

Dad, God bless him, granted her wish and took her tired old body back to Ramsgate. Anything else would have been unthinkable. She was part of the very soil of the place; she loved it with a fierce possessiveness, and she passed that love on to me. When I die I too would like to be taken back to Ramsgate so that either my bones will feed my native soil or my smoke and ashes will dance in the air above the town.

Four

When Dad took Grandma's body home for burial and saw Ramsgate again, bruised and battered, its streets lacking houses here and there like missing teeth, it drew him back. Within months we had all followed her home and settled with Grandpa in their old house, which seemed to have shrunk mysteriously during our absence.

The war was almost over. VE Day arrived, and the shabby little town shook its ruffled feathers and began rebuilding. After the horror of the atomic bombs on Japan came VJ Day, and the end was truly here.

Mum and Dad, always in their element when faced with a challenge, worked like beavers, throwing away some of Grandma's worm-eaten furniture and saving what was still decent for the front basement parlour, which was turned into a bed-sitting room for Grandpa. I was given a room to myself for the first time in my life – after all I was fourteen, almost grown up and having periods.

I joined the local library, the youth club and once again enrolled for evening classes, but once again it was not to be. Dad was setting up a few deals back in Merrie England – another bingo stall, a darts stall and part shares in some pinball machines – and I was included in his plans.

The following Easter Merrie England opened its doors once more, trying to recapture the splendour of the pre-war years. It was all very different. The freak shows had gone, replaced by optical illusions. The Decapitated Lady and the Forsaken Mermaid revealed two local girls, one whose head rested on a powderpuff which, with the use of mirrors, seemed to float in space, the other reclining on a seashell in a fishtail and a pink body stocking, a long yellow wing glued across her meagre tits. Both of them stared indolently at the punters. Chewing gum and bored, lacking the mystery of their predecessors who had gone for good.

As for me, the years in Blackpool had taught me a great deal. Though only fifteen, I was as good a grafter as any of the experienced old barkers who came down from London every season. I looked trustworthy and innocent, and was always sent out to humour the teams of drunken day-trippers who arrived in coachloads from London. But it had lost its magic for me – being part of that brand of grafters, working twelve hours a day, seven days a week, had lost its thrill.

I wanted to be one of the holidaymakers now, free to lounge on the beach during the day, to dress up and go out in the evenings with my friends, instead of being stuck on the darts stall, calling out until my throat hurt, 'Here you are, sir! Three darts for sixpence, Come on, sir, be a sport! Win a prize for your girlfriend', while I smiled at some old codger who obviously had his wife on his arm. Flattering and cajoling some poor bugger out of his hard-earned wages. 'Oh bad luck, sir! Once more for luck?' – the most overused words to fall from my insincere lips. The moral values of fairground life were strange. Dad's pride in a daughter smart enough to relieve a poor punter of his holiday money changed into Quaker-like prudery should a boy linger too long at the stall.

Nevertheless I stuck it out. I was an obedient daughter and, for all Dad's sternness, he was a good protective father. But a slavedriver he certainly was, and a work-aholic. 'Hard work never killed anybody' was his maxim, and in my case he was out to prove it. My brothers seemed to escape the drudgery completely. They were never expected to do household tasks and enjoyed a pretty care-free existence, which led to a growing resentment on my part as the outside world beckoned seductively.

During the winter months I wasn't allowed to be idle. I

took whatever work I could get from October to Easter. One year I was a Woolworth's girl, which I didn't mind. It was child's play after working for Dad. By 1947, during my sixteenth year, things began to light up after the years of darkness and denial. Make-up started to appear in the shops – cyclamen lipsticks in cardboard cases, real nail varnish that didn't peel off, perfume (Evening in Paris and Californian Poppy were the most popular). And Max Factor's pancake make-up, which had to be applied with a wet sponge, giving our smooth young complexions a masklike finish, and blue eyeshadow were worn by all and sundry. Rodgers and Hammerstein's *Oklahoma!*, with 'Oh What a Beautiful Morning' epitomized the feeling of newness and rebirth all round.

I made lots of friends during the first years in Ramsgate. One was Pat, who went to the same youth club and lived in the next street. Pat was what could only be described as 'a good girl'. She never let boys go any further than a chaste kiss.

And there was my cousin Marion, who wasn't. To begin with Marion was more of a pest than a friend, as no one who has reached the age of sixteen can have much in common with someone three years her junior. She was really my second cousin. Grandma's brother's daughter. After his first wife died her father, Uncle Jack, had married a woman over twenty years his junior and Marion was the offspring. At the beginning of the war her mother fell for a soldier and ran off with him, leaving Marion in the care of her father, who was skipper of the Ramsgate lifeboat. She was put into an orphanage as her father was unable to care for her, and subjected to the same kind of mistreatment that I had suffered at Nanny Bridget's hands. After two years she was taken away from there by her father and put into the care of several foster parents. She was quickly passed from pillar to post, and she was by now a very disturbed child, wanting only the security of her own father's presence. Finally in despair he kept her with him, and for the rest of the war years she ran wild in the tunnels, lice-ridden and happy, in the care of anyone who would keep an eye on her while her father was at sea. He was a hero of Dunkirk and received a medal for saving 2800 men from the beaches.

At the end of the war her mother came home, bringing with her a son by the soldier, and set up an unhappy household with Marion and her father. But it was too late to make amends. Marion was a rebel, full of resentment against her mother, and fiercely possessive of her father, whom she adored with the same devotion I had shown to Grandma. But he, totally dependent on his wife for the upbringing of Marion and her little half-brother, sided more and more with her in the face of Marion's rebelliousness and jealousy, and Marion sought refuge in the safety and normality of our home.

This was not to my liking. She haunted me, ingratiating herself to become a part of my life and share my grown-up friends. For ages she was a thorn in my side. 'Here comes your bloody cousin,' Pat would say, and we'd dive down side streets running like the wind to get away from her. But she was family, and eventually, as the years narrowed the gap between us, we became inseparable, our lives interwoven with extraordinary adventures.

She was a pretty child, and now is a beautiful woman, with dark Romany looks from her father's side of the family. To date she has five marriages behind her and high hopes for the future.

My teen years were packed with incident. Fashion followed fashion, each one pursued with empty-headed and relentless devotion, from bobby sox to bebop. The American post-war invasion arrived, and we were pursued and won over with gifts of nylons and Hershey bars. I wore my cardigan back to front and turned into Lana Turner overnight. My virginity was protected by my anxious father, who struck fear into the heart of any would-be seducer.

I left work on the darts stall and got a job as a walkie snap photographer, wading into the mobs of day-trippers and conning them into having group photos taken. 'How about a nice souvenir of your day out, boys? And what about one for the girlfriend? A nice enlargement apiece?' I could sell ice-cream to the Eskimos. But in the winters it was back to the menial boring jobs, because I didn't have the qualifications to land a decent job. I was only street smart.

Then Grandpa became ill. Cancer developed in the antrim under his left eye and spread rapidly. There was no question of sending him to hospital. Mum and Dad nursed him lovingly at home. We children were in and out of his room, while he sat up in bed, his eyes still twinkling over the bandages, conveying his needs with a bony finger – more coal on the fire, the radio on or off. And when he wanted peace he would draw a circle in the air and jab his finger at the door as a signal for us to 'piss orf'. He died while I was at work one day, and by the time I arrived home all traces of him had gone. Even the bed had been taken away and the room scrubbed clean to remove all traces of the sickly smell of cancer, which all my mother's efforts had never been quite able to erase. He was a gentle old man, needing little from life, acquiring nothing. He left behind the princely sum of £11, not much for someone who had slaved on the trawlers all his life.

Not long after Grandpa died Dad sold the house. He was sick of the fairground life, the hard summers and the lean winters. He bought a house with shop premises right in the main street and went into the fish business, selling speciality foods like home-smoked fish, lobsters and dressed crabs.

I was happy to leave the fairground but sad to leave the house and all its memories. But the outside world was calling. I was eighteen years old and hanging on to my virginity by the skin of my teeth. The most favoured contestants were the handsome Americans who flocked into Ramsgate. Many of my girlfriends had already been won over, some were engaged; but in spite of the GIs' looks and glamour, I hadn't lost my heart.

I had a friend from my youth-club days, another Joan, who was dating one of the fairground barkers from Margate's amusement park. She talked me into my first blind date. It was a Londoner who had come down to work in the fairground for the season. Her description of him was so compelling that my curiosity was aroused. We all arranged to meet at the bus stop at Ramsgate harbour. It was a bright evening in early summer and I was nervous with anticipation. My date was standing on the platform as the bus pulled in, and as it slowed to a halt he leaped off. At my first sight of him, suspended as he seemed in mid-air, I knew why nobody else had won my heart. Fate had reserved it for him.

He was all the things I hadn't known I wanted. Firstly, he was gorgeous. Tall and dark, with green eyes full of warmth and humour. Second, he was funny and charm oozed out of him in all directions. But last and by no means least, he loved poetry. I was devastated. By the end of the evening he had me on my back under the trees in Pegwell Bay, trying to get into my knickers as he quoted Andrew Marvell – 'Had we but world enough, and time . . .' I was literally hard-pressed, but training and fear kept my 'well-preserved virginity' intact.

Two more dates followed in rapid succession, two more poetry-filled nights, with him pulling all his stops out, me demanding he put them in again, until indeed 'into ashes went his lust' and on the fourth date the bounder stood me up.

Did I blame him? Not for one moment. I blamed myself. I should have let him have his way – he had certainly tried hard enough. After waiting by the harbour bus stop for over an hour, my heart slowly shrinking as the minutes ticked away, I dragged my way homewards, hoping against hope that I would hear his voice behind me. 'Sorry I kept you waiting. The bus crashed.' But I didn't see him again for four long years. However, he stayed in my heart and my dreams. His memory kept vigil on my tear-soaked pillow. Had I but known, my tears were unnecessary.

★

When the tear-soaked pillow dried I was up and about again. At eighteen one doesn't die from love, there are far too many other things to be doing and far too many people to do them with.

I was relieved of my virginity by the handsome son of a millionaire on his daddy's yacht in Ramsgate harbour. After losing my first love by holding on to my virtue, I wasn't about to let that happen again. It wasn't a great romance, but a consoling one. I can't remember how it ended or why.

Not long after losing heart and hymen, I landed a job as a dental nurse. I couldn't believe my luck. To me this was a step up in the world. The dental practice was situated in Broadstairs, a rather snobbish little town, renowned for the fact that my hero Charles Dickens had lived there and wrote many of his books in various houses, the most famous of them being Bleak House, which stand above the pretty little harbour. Although Broadstairs is a mere three miles from Ramsgate, it was inhabited by a totally different class of people from those I had previously been accustomed to working among. Here I met posh people on a regular basis and held their hands and calmed their fears. In return I was treated with respect. I picked up the work like lightning, cheerfully mopping up blood and vomit, my years of dealing with people on the fairground proving an asset. I kept quiet about my past, however, and I certainly didn't want it to be known at work that Dad had a fish shop in Ramsgate and that I worked there most evenings during the summer months dishing out jellied eels and pie and mash.

I was eager to improve myself and went to yet another set of evening classes to study shorthand and typing. I began to speak in a more refined way, wanting desperately to be accepted in a higher stratum of society than my own. The fact that being a dental nurse was a dead-end job and that the work itself was boring didn't occur to me for ages. The drawbacks were overshadowed by the opportunity it gave me to meet all those grand Broadstairs residents.

Then I met an art student called Jacques and we immediately became inseparable. I was his first love, he was my second. We made love wherever and whenever possible, mostly in caves or on the sands behind a stack of deck chairs. But his mother, a chic Parisienne, had plans for her son's future that didn't include me and she arrived in Ramsgate to take him home. We wrote to each other for a time, but my letters must have been intercepted and his finally ceased.

A year later I became engaged to a tall, blond master sergeant from Virginia. He drove a big flashy car and completely turned my head. I was taken to restaurants, dances and eventually to London for a dirty weekend in a smart hotel. On arriving home I found Jacques waiting for me. He was wearing scruffy black clothes, with a rip in the seat of his pants, bare feet in open sandals and long hair. He had rebelled completely, run away from home and become an existentialist. He had taken a room in Montmartre, where he was scraping a living as an artist, and he wanted me to share it with him.

But I couldn't run off and live like a gypsy; I had lived like one for a large part of my life and it held no glamour for me. I wanted comfort and respectability. I made my choice and went back to the consoling arms of my American.

A few months later he was recalled to America. It was only to be for a short time, he said, promising to return with the marriage licence. I never saw him again. However, he did leave something of himself behind, and while I waited expectantly for his return, my horror at his treachery growing, I discovered that I was pregnant.

I kept the dreadful secret from my parents as long as I dared, praying that he would come back and rescue me. When I finally confessed, to my surprise there were no recriminations. 'You poor little bugger,' said Dad. 'It's our problem now,' said Mum. Dad said it would be nice to have a 'bab' in the house. But I knew that if I went through with this birth I would be tied to my parents by poverty and gratitude for the rest of my life.

I made inquiries and found the address of a London abortionist who charged £4 and did it in her home. She lived in Brixton and I set off one morning by coach, my parents thinking I was at work. The woman was unsympathetic and nervous. She said it wasn't convenient just then, her husband would be back soon and he didn't know about what she did. I pleaded with her, saying that I had come all the way from Ramsgate. I showed her the money. 'We'll have to be quick about it then,' she said, and took me into the kitchen. I was made to crouch over a bowl of soapy water while she pushed an enema syringe into my womb, filling it to expel the little life that was holding on so tenaciously. A large old mongrel dog surveyed the grisly scene with a sympathetic eye, and I held on to its neck for comfort and support. I wasn't allowed any time to recover but was hustled out after parting with my £4.

On the way home the pains began: they grew in intensity until by the time I arrived home I was in agony. Mother knew immediately what I had done and put me straight to bed where I aborted a baby boy. Dad never spoke of it to me.

A few days later I was back at work pleading a bad cold, my secret safe. There was nothing to show for that small life lost. My first lesson in comeuppance was bitterly learned.

Five

Coronation Year – 1953 – arrived. The second Elizabethan era – a good omen, everyone said. Although things were still short and food still rationed, England was perking up. Television was appearing in the homes of the few who could afford it, Mr J. Arthur Rank was breathing life into the British Film Industry and American musicals were brightening up our days.

My cousin Marion had emigrated to America and was living in California. Her letters were full of wonder at the many marvellous opportunities to be found there and she urged me to join her, but leaving England was out of the question.

I was twenty-two, and although I was holding down the same boring job I had a flat which I shared with a girl-friend, Mary, a nurse at Margate hospital. One weekend Mary and I went to Margate for the day, and as we were walking through Dreamland amusement park I met my first love again. He was working another season in the fairground. The intervening years had done nothing to diminish his attractiveness. In fact, he was more gorgeous than ever and my stomach lurched as I looked up into his green eyes. In the space of five minutes we had made a date for that same night. This time things were on a more equal footing – I had some poetry of my own.

Douglas stayed the night, and practically every night after that until we were married two months later. It wasn't really a whirlwind romance. After all, I had waited four years for him and the second time I wasn't going to let him go.

He borrowed £15 and bought a second-hand navy-blue pinstripe suit for the wedding. My parents gave us £50, and I bought a green tweed suit and a dreadful black hat with feathers sweeping down one side of my face. Aunt May and Uncle Harry gave us a pair of blankets. My boss, the dentist, gave us a pressure cooker and let me take Saturday morning off to get married. He also asked me not to tell any of the patients that I was getting married – he wanted me to go on being Miss Long.

Douglas and I were married at Ramsgate registry office on Saturday, 23 October 1953. Mum and Dad gave us a wedding party with a crab and lobster buffet. Douglas, who was an abstainer, drank tea and the rest of my family and friends got tiddly. After the reception we went to our cheap rented flat, I with a bad headache and Douglas with a raging toothache. We didn't make love on our wedding night, and on the Monday morning I went to work and he went to a dentist in Ramsgate to have his tooth fixed. Somehow it didn't seem appropriate to take him to mine.

Although our married life was marred by poverty, we had much in common. For a start we were each other's best friend. We had no need for anyone else. We even shared the same books (library, of course), reading aloud to each other or talking into the small hours most nights. There was enormous affection between us, lots of hugging and kissing, until it got serious, and then I would cry off. I don't know why, but with marriage the glamour had gone. For me making love became one of the nightly tasks, like washing or brushing my teeth, and there was always the same feeling of sadness when it was over. Mercifully it didn't diminish our love and friendship. In those days orgasms weren't talked of as they are now, and, unbelievable as it seems, I had never heard of them, let alone had one. As far as I was concerned I certainly couldn't miss what I hadn't had.

But there were many things absent from the life of my husband which he did miss. He had been brought up in grinding poverty. At one stage of his childhood the whole family – including four children – had been forced to live in one room. The school he went to as a child was another Victorian abomination which carried over the gateway in letters of stone the welcoming words 'The Ragged School', and because of their situation the family was given a jug of hot soup, which Douglas had to collect and take home every day after school. But whereas poverty had turned me into a dreamer, it had made Douglas angry and rebellious. He became a socialist. His parents, who were strict Catholics, despaired of him, as he had also turned his back on religion.

Douglas was very proud, and back in the fifties, when most employers behaved like little dictators, he found it hard to keep his cap in his hand and his pride in his pocket. Uncle Harry got him his first job in the packing department at a local plastics factory. It was menial, boring work, but it brought in £6 10s a week, which, along with my £4 from the dental practice, was not to be sneezed at in those days. Douglas hated the work and would come home in the evenings simmering with suppressed rage at the rudeness of his foreman and the subservience of his fellow employees.

The week before Christmas the boss, a Mr Cole, came to the factory to deliver a pep talk. The men were assembled before him as he berated them about their slovenliness, lack of enthusiasm and bad workmanship, ending with the chilling warning that if standards were no better in the coming year, heads would roll. In the silence that followed Douglas's voice rang out loud and clear. 'Thank you very much, Mr Cole. Come round any time, we'll be glad to put you on the fire.' He was sacked on the spot.

A job as a painter and decorator came vacant. He was hired, great joy followed and we made plans as to what we would do with the first week's wages – £10. When he turned up for work on his first morning he was told to sit in a cradle suspended over the cliffs and paint iron safety girders.

'Are you kidding?' asked Douglas in horror. 'I suffer from vertigo.'

'More like a touch of cowardice, if you ask me,' said the foreman. Douglas picked him up by the lapels.

There were many instances like that. I didn't blame him. He simply couldn't take that particular brand of authority. He drew unemployment benefit of £2 5s. a week and somehow we scraped by. After rent we had £3 a week on which to feed and clothe ourselves. The pressure cooker saved our lives. On Mondays in went the remains of Sunday's joint with a few vegetables, and we ate out of that through the week, adding bits and pieces as we could afford them.

'What's for dinner tonight, dear?' was the daily question.

'A four-letter word beginning with S,' I would reply.

'Shit again?' he'd say.

Nevertheless we were happy enough: there were few disagreements between us and our needs were small. We never drank and our main pleasure was the cinema. Once a week in the 1s 9d seats was all we could afford. Long walks and library books cost nothing, and we were never bored with each other. The only cloud was his frustration. 'I know there's something I can do well, but I can't find what it is,' he would say. He tried painting, poetry, writing. A friend lent him a guitar and he learned how to play. Then, on one of his painting and decorating jobs, he was given a piano. He was getting warmer. Within a year he was playing in a pub during the winter evenings, earning a few pounds on the side singing and playing the old standards. He wasn't bad and his looks were a great asset.

In the summers he went back to the fairground. His London friends came down for the season. That was fun for us both, and the money he earned helped us through the lean winters. One summer he managed to save £100.

The money came in handy because at this time Mum and Dad moved to Luton with my brothers. There were good wages to be earned in the car factories, which were having a post-war boom. We rented their house in Ramsgate for 30s. a week. Somehow we managed to furnish our first real home out of that £100. We were broke again but happy.

Another winter passed. Nothing changed except my job. In five years my wages had risen by only 5s. a week, and since my marriage I had grown discontented. I still smarted from my employer's disapproval of Douglas, whom he thought of as a fairground layabout.

'Just leave,' Doug would say.

'But how will we live?'

'We'll get by,' he assured me. 'Don't worry about the future. There's no point in making yourself unhappy.'

'Someone's got to worry about it,' said the echo of my mother.

'OK, then I'll worry for you one hour a day.'

He wanted to come to the surgery and give notice for me, but I begged him, in tears, not to embarrass me. Besides, I needed a good reference and I wouldn't have got that if my husband had been moved to pick the dentist up by his lapels. My farewell gift after five years' hard slog was 10s. extra in my pay packet.

Douglas claimed for me on the National Assistance – £1 extra a week. The hired radio (2s 6d a week) went back. The cinema treat now took place about once a month. I stood over the pressure cooker like one of the witches in *Macbeth*, stirring away to make it yield sufficient sustenance. After coal, rent, money for the gas meter, there was £1 a week left on which to feed ourselves. The pleasure of lying in his arms as long as I wanted to in the mornings was marred by the fact that there was seldom any breakfast to get out of bed for. This poverty was no bohemian joke.

I eventually got a job in a guest house, serving breakfast, cleaning bedrooms and going back in the evenings to do the dinners. We saved like squirrels, which was all to the good because that autumn, 1956, I became pregnant.

I was overjoyed. It was the happiest time of my life to

date. But for Douglas things became more serious. Now he was the one to worry.

'How will we manage with another mouth to feed?'

'Don't worry – he'll be breast-fed. Babies don't cost much,' I said placidly.

But Douglas did worry. 'I've got to make something of myself. I can't bring a kid up in poverty.'

He went back to the fairground that summer, working in Merrie England to be close at hand for the birth. He was the most wonderful expectant father, indulging all my cravings, which were for oranges, Mint Imperials and Gorgonzola cheese.

On the morning of 9 June 1957 I went into labour, after having gone for a ride on the pillion of my brother David's motorbike (he was visiting us from Luton). Doug took me to Ramsgate hospital in a taxi. As we were driving along the harbour parade a Salvation Army band came out of a side street, and we were escorted up the hill to the hospital accompanied by the strains of 'Pomp and Circumstance'.

'Our kid is going to be somebody,' Doug said with tears in his eyes.

Our son David was born at 8.30 the following night, and as soon as I saw him I felt as if I had known him for ever. He was long and skinny, with masses of dark hair. Motherhood is a strange and magical experience. One minute I had a bump and suddenly here was someone for whom I would gladly have faced a firing squad.

Douglas ran all the way from Merrie England to the hospital after the phone call telling him he had a son. It was what we had both prayed for.

It was while I was in hospital that Douglas decided what he wanted to do. The previous winter he had joined the local amateur dramatic group. They were planning to put on Christopher Fry's *The Lady's Not for Burning* but couldn't find a Thomas Mendip, until they saw Douglas.

He was a born actor; he looked wonderful in tights. The local papers raved about him, saying that he had a natural gift, that he should be a professional, and so on. He loved it, and the seed was sown. That autumn he left for London to try his luck in the hard and hazardous profession of acting, while I settled down contentedly with my son.

Doug's sister Kathy was at the Rose Bruford Drama College and she gave him a lot of help – names of teachers, tips on stage make-up, how to walk across a stage – and, armed with this and grafter's bluff, not to mention his handsome appearance, he went the rounds of the agents' offices.

Within a short space of time he had landed a TV commercial. It wasn't much to write home about, though he did, with great pride and excitement. He played the part of a house painter standing on a scaffold and had to knock a tin of paint over Jon Pertwee, who then said, 'It covers me completely, and such a smooth finish.' Sadly, when the commercial was released only Doug's foot was in the picture. He said it was a good omen, starting feet first.

He found himself an agent, who changed his name, thinking that Douglas Malin was too ordinary. I was sorry about that. I thought that Mark Eden sounded a bit unreal; I still do, but it's too late now over thirty years later. And so Mark Eden began his career. He bluffed his way into Swansea Rep and embarked upon a new life, finding his much-needed fulfilment. From there he went to Nottingham Rep and fell in love with an actress.

I knew the marriage was over before he told me, though I didn't want to believe it. But when he confessed that he was in love I knew that there was nothing I could do. You can't command someone to love you. It was all over bar the crying, and there was a lot of that in the months that followed. We stayed friends though. We liked each other a great deal. We had always been more like brother and sister than husband and wife and we had David as a bond between us.

Doug did what he could for David and me, though it wasn't much. They were lean years. I couldn't work with a toddler on my hands, so in desperation I moved to Luton to join my family. The unhappiest time of my life followed. Mum looked after David while I got a fascinating job in a ballbearing factory. I stood in tears at the bus stop every morning, cursing the actress and Mark Eden, Luton and the ballbearing factory, and wondering if I was going to be condemned to a life sentence in this awful place.

David was my salvation. He was the most joyful child in the history of children. He never whined, he slept when he was put down to sleep, and he smiled away my blues. At least my marriage had yielded up this blessing. I couldn't stay in Luton, the hopelessness of it was killing my spirit.

The power-mad chargehand who ruled over the portion of assembly belt where I worked gave me a roasting for taking too long in the lavatory one day. It was the final straw. 'When the foreman tells me how long I can take to have a crap, it's time I left,' and I swept out of the place with a light heart. I decided there and then that I would never work in a factory again.

I went back to Ramsgate and threw myself on to the meagre charity of the Welfare State. The means test was nothing compared with the indignity of having one's bowel movements timed. Three pounds a week was the sum granted me by a worthy gentleman who treated me as if I'd just returned from a leper colony. But I bit my tongue and took the money.

My cousin Marion arrived home from America with her second husband, James. They moved in with me, accompanied by a poodle and her five puppies, a record player and a stack of the latest sounds from the States, and trunks full of beautiful clothes. After the austerity of the previous years, it was like living in Aladdin's cave. Marion's clothes filled my wardrobe and she insisted that I share them with her. Until then my entire wardrobe occupied four hangers and my skirts shone with the patina of age and constant pressing. Now suddenly I was swanning around Ramsgate in the latest fashions.

Marion did me over. She had trained as a beautician in America. She cut my hair into a short, ragged style which suited me, plucked my eyebrows and showed me how to make up. More importantly, she and James brought fun back into my life, and self-esteem.

Not long after they arrived my welfare cheque stopped. I was summoned to the Broadstairs office and grilled by the sadist who had carried out my means test. 'It has come to my notice,' he said, looking at me over the top of his glasses, 'that you have people living in your house of a suspicious nature. People have been seen leaving late at night. Music has been heard and you are suddenly sporting a lot of new clothes. I should like an explanation.' He was practically accusing me of living on immoral earnings.

I tried to explain about Marion, the old friends who hadn't seen her for some years, the clothes. The bastard didn't even listen. 'I still have reason to believe that you have money coming in from other sources, and I am cancelling your National Assistance benefit as from now,' he said. And that was the end of the matter.

'Never mind,' said Marion when I arrived home boiling with indignation, 'he probably wears a pinny at home while his wife smacks his bare bum with a carpet beater.'

We were really on the breadline now, however. James and Marion may have had lots of lovely things, but hard cash to buy food with was another matter. Marion got a part-time job in an antiques shop which brought in £2. 12s 6d a week. When she got paid we bought the week's food for David and the dogs, and what was left over was for us. Breast of lamb on Sundays, and out came the pressure cooker for the rest of the week. Come summer James and I found work running the box office of the Pavilion Theatre, while Marion stayed at home to look after David.

It was my first encounter with theatrical people and I was fascinated by them, from the star, Reg ('Confidentially') Dixon, who took a liking to James and me, to the chorus girls and stage hands. They were all so warm and friendly that when they left at the end of the season it was as if the lights had gone out over Ramsgate.

Not long after that Marion and James moved to London, leaving such a gap in my life that the house seemed to echo with emptiness. I had made three friends that summer who mercifully kept in touch and who came down to see me from time to time – Peter Dixon, a singer, his friend Jeffrey, both gay, and a girl of my age, Beau, whose friendship has lasted throughout all these years. They all urged me to get out of Ramsgate and join them in London, and although I knew that David would have a more settled life if I resigned myself to staying there, I wanted to be part of what was going on. Mum and Dad solved my problem by moving back to Ramsgate and they offered to take care of David. And so, knowing that he would be well loved and promising to come home every weekend, I left for London.

Six

In the following five years so many things happened, so many changes took place, that I see that time as a multi-coloured ball of wool in a tangle, with little to connect one event to the next but a mere strand of coincidence. I could pull a dozen stories out of that tangle, some good, some bad, but each one exciting. I was living at last. I was out there doing it as opposed to reading about it in a library book or listening to it on a rented radio.

By 1963 I had changed jobs at least four times and lived in a succession of bed-sitters, and I shall pick up a thread here, because it ultimately leads, albeit circuitously, to my first meeting with the person who was to be the one unchanging and reliable influence in my life – John Le Mesurier, who became my second husband. I was working as a clerk at Marylebone labour exchange in Lisson Grove and living directly opposite, renting a room in a flat belonging to Peter Dixon and his mother, Dorothy.

A more unlikely candidate for a job in the Civil Service would be hard to imagine. My work consisted of signing in and stamping the cards of the casual workers who in those days were required to come to the labour exchange each day they were out of work. Most of my clients were actors, some quite well-known faces, others were stunt men or extras, and though I say it myself, they couldn't have been in better hands. At the start of my working day I was issued with a franking stamp, which I had to sign for every morning and sign back in at night, and which I had to carry wherever I went in a little bag which hung on my wrist. It was literally worth its weight in gold because one stamp on a card represented a day's pay for someone.

Pay days were traumatic occasions. There were always those unfortunates who found nothing waiting for them in their paypackets. Fights broke out regularly and sometimes the police had to be called. It was a battleground, with all sorts of people having to wait in line for their money, some drunk, some angry and rebellious, others deeply embarrassed at being subjected to this method of claiming what was rightly theirs.

In order to supplement my income I took a second job working in the bar at the Queen's Theatre, Shaftesbury Avenue, five nights a week. At first I thought that the extra work would kill me, especially when there were matinées, which meant I had to rush to the theatre straight from work to catch the interval trade. The show was *Stop the World, I Want to Get Off*, a huge hit. Antony Newley was the star and every night, after the interval rush, I would stand at the back to watch him sing 'Gonna Build a Mountain'. I never did get to see the whole show.

After work I would occasionally meet Beau for a drink. She had lived in St Martin's Lane all her life, and as a child would hang around stage doors watching the stars come and go with the same devotion and dedication that I had spent bunking in through the back door of the Lyric cinema. But whereas my childhood had been full of fantasy, hers was rooted in the colour and energy of the real thing. There wasn't a show she hadn't seen or a name she didn't know, and she rounded off my education and showed me a London that I would never have found without her.

Her favourite haunt was the Fifty Club in Frith Street, Soho. It was owned by a married couple called Johnny and Patsy. They presented a total contrast. Johnny was handsome and elegantly dressed, with the bearing of a gentleman and a public-school accent. Patsy was Jewish and flamboyant, given to wearing elaborate hats, and she had an accent that would slip slightly if she had put down one glass of champers too many. She always sat on the customer's side of the bar. She could spot phoneys or troublemakers the instant they entered the room, and if she took a dislike to someone, he was removed by Johnny faster than the speed of sound. They were a formidable duo.

The club was famous among the acting profession and Beau was a close friend and welcome guest. I counted myself honoured to be permitted to tread this hallowed ground. It was one of the few places we could go without a male escort, protected and safe under the watchful eyes of our hosts.

One particular night stands out in my memory as a turning point in my life. I arrived at the club as usual to find Beau deep in conversation with a man who, with his clipped delivery and stern, piercing eyes, on first impression bore a remarkable likeness to the actor Clifton Webb. His name was Johnny Heawood and he was a choreographer of some note, responsible for shows like *The Boy Friend* and *Irma la Douce*; he had also assisted on the film of *Guys and Dolls*. He was captivating: Canadian, gay and wickedly humorous. He told us that although he didn't like the girls as a rule, he liked us. After several drinks he suddenly said, 'How would you two gorgeous dames like to have a drink at the Establishment?'

Now the Establishment Club in those days was just about as 'in' as you could get. It was the centre of the revival of real political satire, fronted by Peter Cook and Dudley Moore, two of the up-and-coming young talents from Cambridge who were enjoying a huge success in a revue called *Beyond the Fringe*. The decor was designed by Sean Kenny and the club was patronized by just about every celebrity of note in the acting profession. The publicity it had attracted was phenomenal. The waiting list for membership was over 5000 and every night there was a queue of people trying to gain admission. I had read about the Establishment and longed to see it, but the chance of ever being invited to it was about as remote as a trip to Mars.

Beau and I stared at Johnny incredulously, her blue eyes

widening like saucers. 'You're joking,' she said. 'You mean *the* Establishment?'

'Where else, dear?' said Johnny. 'The man who runs the joint is an old friend of mine,' and off we went, Beau and I still wearing our barmaids' black, to Greek Street, where we were escorted through the crowd and in through the doors of the most famous nightclub in London. Johnny led us to the bar, our heads on swivels as we took in the famous decor and the well-known faces dotted among the crowd, and introduced us to the manager, Bruce Copp.

'Who's in tonight, dear?' asked Johnny.

'John Le Mesurier's watching the show, but he'll be out any minute now,' said Bruce, and left us to attend to business.

'You must meet my dear friend John,' said Heawood.

'Who's John Le Mesurier?' I asked.

'Don't you know who John Le Mesurier is?' said Beau. 'He's a lovely character actor. He's in practically every English comedy.' She reeled off a list of films in which he had appeared.

'You'll know his face when you see him,' said Heawood. And indeed I did, as soon as he came ambling towards us.

'My dear fellow,' said John, patting Heawood on the back. 'How nice to see you.' We were introduced, and for the first time I looked into the kind brown eyes of the man who for the next twenty-two years was to bring to my life great depth of experience and a deep abiding love.

During the evening we all went to the basement to hear the Dudley Moore Trio. Before the set Dudley came over to talk to John. He took my hand and asked if I had a favourite song, and when I asked him if he knew a number called 'What's New', John raised his eyebrows.

'How does a slip of a girl like you know an old song like that?' he asked. 'It happens to be my favourite.'

I told him that, along with my passion for poetry, I also loved the lyrics of the old torch songs and ballads and could reel them off *ad infinitum*. It turned out that he was fanatical about modern jazz. He loved all music and felt himself to be a frustrated musician at least. 'Perhaps when someone special comes to Ronnie Scott's Club, you might like to come with me, my little friend,' he said. It might not seem much on which to base a lifetime's companionship, but the tenuous bond proved that we were on the same wavelength in one small way.

The idea of any sort of relationship with him never crossed my mind at that first meeting, nor did it for a long time to come. I simply saw him as a gentle, fatherly man who in spite of his biting humour, had an air of sadness about him. I wasn't attracted to older men. In fact my preference at that time was for dissolute young actors or men who had problems. Show me some screwed-up good-looking ne'er do well in those days and my eyes would light up.

At the end of the evening we thanked Bruce for his hospitality and were told that any time we would like to return to the club we had only to ask for him at the door. Then John took us home, depositing me at my door in a gentlemanly fashion. I had made three new friends and been given plenty of food for thought.

Unbeknown to me, at that first casual meeting with John wheels had already begun to turn behind the scenes, set in motion by the clever Mr Copp, who, having known John for years, could see that he was taken by me. At the time of our meeting, John had been married for twelve years to Hattie Jacques, the well-loved and talented actress and comedienne. Their marriage, blessed by two sons, was reputed to be one of the most successful in show business, and so it had been until the year before John and I first met.

Hattie was deeply involved in charity work, her two favourite causes being Leukemia and the Spastics' Society, for which she toiled selflessly. She didn't drive, so a volunteer driver would take her to various fund-raising activities.

One night her usual driver was unobtainable and a

newcomer stepped in at the last moment. Steve had just joined the Leukemia Society because his own child, a two-year-old boy, had recently died of the disease. Hattie's heart went out to him and he became her permanent driver. It later came to light that his marriage was in trouble. Hattie became his confidante and friend, and eventually they became lovers. By the time I met John this situation had been going on for a year, and although John didn't realize – or didn't want to accept – what was happening, he was growing increasingly unhappy about the constant presence of this man in his home.

Hattie and Steve, by now desperate to be together openly, knew that the only way John would ever leave was if he fell for another woman. So seeing John's interest in me, Bruce, who had been a close friend of Hattie's for many years, decided to do a bit of matchmaking.

The following week I received an invitation to go to the Establishment again with Beau and Heawood, who was also in on the conspiracy. I readily accepted. Bruce greeted Beau and me like long-lost sisters and invited us to go with him to Hattie's; she was giving a little supper party that evening, John would be there and would very much like to see us again. To be absolutely honest, I would have much preferred to stay right where I was, but Heawood and Bruce appeared so eager to have our company that it seemed churlish to refuse.

However, unwittingly I was a sorry disappointment to anyone hoping to lead me straight into poor John's arms, because before we left the club we were joined by a newcomer who was right up my street. A Canadian actor, Bill was smooth-talking and untidy, with trouble written as plain as day across his forehead. Johnny Heawood's warning, 'If you want my advice, dear, run for your life from this hunk,' only whetted my appetite. By the time we left Bill had insinuated himself into our party and my heart was beating eight to the bar.

There were quite a few people at Hattie's when we arrived, and as I entered the room my eye fell on a handsome man who bore a striking resemblance to Cary Grant.

'Who is that?' I asked Heawood.

'That,' Heawood answered, 'is *taboo*.'

'That,' of course, was Steve, but at the time I didn't know what was going on and, besides, I was with Bill. Heawood introduced me to Hattie, who was so warm and friendly that I felt I had known her for years. Within a short space of time I was telling her about my marriage, my jobs and how I came to be in London. I asked her if she had any children. 'Three,' she answered, 'and John is the youngest.'

Later I joined John, who patted my shoulder and said, 'Hello, my little friend.' We looked through his record collection together and discussed our favourite singers. He looked so sad and morose that Beau and I stayed with him and did our best to cheer him up. I asked him about his sons. 'Would you like to meet them?' he asked. 'The little rotters are awake in the next room. They refuse to go to sleep when we have a party.'

Both the boys were sitting up in their beds. Robin the elder, who was about ten at the time, had just been given a bicycle for his birthday. Kim, an adorable, impish child said to me, 'How would you feel if your brother had got a bike and wouldn't let you share it?'

'Very jealous,' I replied.

'What do you do?' asked Robin.

'I'm a private detective,' I answered, 'and I also write ghost stories under an assumed name.'

'Honest?' said Kim.

'Cross my heart, but keep it to yourselves about the detective work because I'm trailing someone at the moment.' I left promising to tell them one of my ghost stories the next time I saw them.

It was a lovely party. In the small hours Hattie disappeared into the kitchen and cooked eggs and bacon for everyone. She was an amazing hostess, tirelessly circulating among her guests, full of energy. I found out where the energy came from when she appeared after supper with a silver salver. 'Purple hearts, anyone?' she said. In those days amphetamines were used freely and easy to obtain. John told me that years before when he was in rep doing two plays a week and two shows a day the only way he found the strength to keep awake and learn his lines was by having a benzedrine pill after supper and working on his script at night.

To Hattie's disappointment, I left the party with Bill. I had given John my phone number and address and, with Hattie's blessing, had promised to go with him to Ronnie Scott's the following week. She told me that she would be delighted for me to keep John company as she seldom had the time and wasn't as mad about jazz as he was.

And so my courtship began. At first John was simply a friend. He never gave me the slightest reason to believe that he regarded me in any other way and I talked as freely to him about my other dates as I would to Beau. Bill proved very early on to be a non-starter, though I saw him from time to time at the Establishment.

By the beginning of the summer of 1963, although I was having a ball living in London, I began to miss my son David so badly that I decided to move back to Ramsgate and spend the summer holidays with him. Fortunately I managed to get myself transferred to Deal labour exchange.

My Dad had gone back into the seafood business and, with a partner, had opened a cafeteria on Ramsgate sea front, which sold every kind of shellfish imaginable, from cockles to lobsters, and was doing a roaring trade. So that I wouldn't be too idle, he had also acquired a stall for me at Ramsgate dogtrack, selling cockles, whelks and jellied eels three nights a week. I didn't mind. It was out in the fresh air and at weekends I could take David with me as he didn't have to get up for school the next morning. It was quite a change from the sophistication of the life I had led in London, but the pleasure of being with my son more than compensated. Beau, who used to spend her summer holidays in Ramsgate when she was a child, often came down to see me for the weekend. She loved the atmosphere at the dogtrack and was quite a gambler. While I was selling my wares she would bring me drinks and place bets. She gave me two tips: during the parade before betting, if a dog has a hard-on or a crap, put your money on it. By some miracle it seemed to work.

By coincidence John and Hattie had a house in Margate. Hattie's mother, Mary, lived there and it was a base for the children during the summer holidays. Occasionally John would come over to visit me and bring Kim to play with David. Once or twice he drove me to the dogtrack, carrying my stock in the boot of his car. He would stand by the stall signing autographs while I worked, and I would send him off to place a bet should a dog make a deposit during the grand parade. It was a strange courtship. We were such an ill-matched pair, but we found a great deal of common ground in our friendship and he made me laugh a lot, in spite of his being almost permanently depressed.

I was also enjoying the fact that, because there was no sexual tension between us, I felt secure with him. I loved his reliability and good manners, and I basked in the respect that being in his company brought when he took me out to dinner or to a bar. I enjoyed the cards he was always sending, which were funny and descriptive. In short, he was becoming a part of my life and his fondness for me was giving me a confidence in myself that I had never experienced until then.

Once or twice during that summer I went to London for the weekend. I usually stayed in my old digs with Peter and Dorothy, and always went to the Establishment with Beau and John to see Bruce and Heawood. During one of these weekends Bruce offered me his flat in St George's Square. Heawood was looking for somewhere to live and Bruce suggested that I should share the flat with Johnny, as long as I took responsibility for the tenancy. Bruce also offered me a job at the Establishment, serving drinks in the ground-floor bar. The hours were long, from eleven at night until three in the morning, but the money was good.

And so that autumn, when the dogtrack closed, I regretfully left David, having arranged to work only every other Saturday night so that I could have alternate long and short weekends with him in Ramsgate, and moved back to London.

Being a workaholic and needing the money, I took a full-time day job at Gibbs Pepsodent in Portman Square, a short bus ride from Pimlico, and settled myself and Heawood into our new quarters.

Johnny was a wonderful flatmate. He was completely irresponsible domestically, which is why Bruce had put me in charge. He showed no interest in food whatsoever and could survive on a plate of spinach or a small herring a day. He was the thinnest man I have ever known, and when I came home from work loaded down with groceries, he would accuse me of having a 'morbid preoccupation with food', although he began to appreciate the fact that there was nearly always something ready for him at night when he came home from the theatre.

He was working at the Players' Theatre at that point. I saw him perform a few times. One of my favourites was a song called 'Sister Rhia', about a little Salvation Army lass who threw her bonnet over the windmill and joined the chorus of a variety show. Heawood danced across the stage as light as air, wearing a Victorian Salvation Army costume, with laced-up boots and granny glasses.

It was also at the Players' Theatre that I saw Hattie, dressed as a little girl, sing 'I Don't Want to Play in Your Yard'. She moved as if she had wheels concealed under her dress. Clive Dunn played the naughty little boy whom she didn't love any more. They were pure enchantment.

The Players' Theatre in Villiers Street was in a class of its own. Known as the Pink Tunnel, it was responsible for giving many talented newcomers a platform in London. Hattie had started her career there, as had Clive Dunn. There were many others – I could fill pages with the names of those who had made their débuts at the Players' Theatre. It was also where, at the end of the war, John, resplendent in captain's uniform, had first seen and fallen in love with Hattie. Sadly but appropriately, it was where we all gathered on the day of Hattie's memorial service many years later.

But to go back to happier times . . . and happy times they were indeed in that winter of 1963. It was happiness which gave me the energy to cram so much activity into my days. I loved every moment, surrounded as I was by interesting, stimulating people, and I floated through my work, kept aloft by some divine energy.

I would get up at 7.30, leave for the office at 8.30, work until five, when I would be met by John, who would take me for a drink or an early dinner, then back to my flat to prepare for work at the Establishment. If I didn't have a date I would go home and rest for a few hours before the night's work. I call it work, and indeed it was hard, but it was rather like going to a party every night. Every well-known face in the business would appear there and visiting celebrities from America, including legendary musicians such as Duke Ellington's trumpet player, Cat Anderson, would come to sit in with the Dudley Moore Trio. I would put down my tray, risking the sack for the thrill of hearing them making music that happened once in a lifetime. Count Basie's band played there; Annie Ross (who was to become a close friend) appeared there in cabaret. Lennie Bruce, Frankie Howerd, Marty Feldman and his wife Lor (who also became special friends of mine) – many fascinating people came through those doors.

That winter was particularly cold, and on the nights I went to Ramsgate I would catch the paper train from London Bridge station at 4.30 in the morning. Before I left the club I would make myself a sandwich and fill a hot-water bottle, and I would settle myself in a first-class compartment to sleep with the bottle strapped to my waist. I was befriended by the guard who always travelled on that train. He would give me a cup of tea and the morning papers and keep an eye on me as I slept, wrapped in my coat and clasping my hot-water bottle to me, with

72

my head on a cushion from the guard's van. When I arrived at Ramsgate a local newsagent, who was waiting for the papers, would give me a lift home. I would let myself in and crawl into bed beside the warm sleepy body of my son.

My weekends were for David alone. It was playtime for us both. Mother tended to treat me as if I were his age as we were always teasing her, particularly when she came out with her oddball remarks such as 'I've only got two pairs of hands' or 'The trouble with antiques is they don't last.' 'What have I said now?' she would ask when she saw us trying to keep our faces straight. We both loved her dearly and I shall always be grateful to her for giving David the foundation of a normal childhood and making it possible for me to have the fling I was having without being riddled by guilt. Even so, those Sunday evening farewells, when David and I both tried to be cheerful and brisk, were the bad time of every week. David told me later that after I had left Mother always tried to cheer him up by saying. 'Ah well, back to the old routine.'

Despite the fact that Douglas – or Mark, as he was now known – had left he still kept in contact with us. Although he was living on the periphery of my life, he was very much at the centre of David's and kept in close touch with his son. He would visit him in Ramsgate whenever he could, and when David stayed with me during the holidays Mark would take him out for treats.

Like me, Mark was having the fling he had missed out on as a young man. It was lovely for each of us, but for our son it was a different matter. He couldn't understand why we didn't live together. One terrible incident which upset all of us happened when I took David to stay with his father for the weekend. Mark had prepared a bed for him and had planned a programme of outings. All went well until the time came for me to leave. David clung to me, begging me to stay too. When we decided that I would take him with me, he hung on to his father. There was no way he could explain to a six-year-old child that our lives had taken separate directions, and in the end I had to carry him home kicking and screaming, leaving Mark, who by this time was also in tears.

There is no magic formula for parenthood. A child is dropped into our lives and is moulded by whatever circumstances exist at the time. Mark and I were both plagued by the knowledge that we should have given David a conventional, stable childhood, but life was too full of temptations and distractions for us to do that. If I suffered a bad conscience at leaving my son on those doom-filled Sunday evenings, Mark, with his Catholic roots, felt a guilt that reached deep down into his soul.

Dear Mark, we could be anything we wanted to others, but we both knew that, in spite of a veneer of sophistication, we were still a couple of snotty-nosed kids who had escaped from our origins by a mixture of bluff and determination. And now, without the responsibility of having to protect each other's egos, we found we could be completely honest with each other. He once asked me if I minded being used as an excuse when one or another of his girlfriends wanted the relationship to be put on a more permanent basis. 'My wife won't give me a divorce' was the reluctant reason for his not tying the knot. Neither of us thought that we would ever marry again – we had breathed the heady air of freedom. Sometimes, when Mark introduced me to his fellow actors as his 'live-out wife', they would ask us how we managed to remain such good friends. The answer is simple: we loved each other – and if love is real it doesn't die; it simply changes.

John and I went to see Mark when he starred in *Night of the Iguana* at the Savoy. The two men liked each other on sight and became friends. This seemed odd to some people – as did the fact that Hattie and I were close – but to me it felt like a growing family.

At the beginning of 1964 Marion came to stay. The arrangement was meant to be purely temporary as she was waiting to join James, who had taken a job in Germany.

Unfortunately she also brought her cat, a two-stone monster called Didiagiar. Heawood hated cats and war was declared between them the moment they met. Matters were not improved when Marion fell in love with a stunt man, a former boxer by the name of Dinny Powell. That signalled the end of her marriage and the temporary arrangement began to look as though it might be permanent. This was too much for Heawood, who issued an ultimatum: either Marion and that damned cat must go or he would. Marion promised to look for somewhere else to live but, before she could find a place, Heawood took matters into his own hands and moved out. I was sorry to see him go; I missed his company. However, Marion was like a sister to me – I couldn't have thrown her out. So there I was with a new ménage – Marion, the cat and, for a greater part of the time, Marion's new boyfriend Dinny.

For John things were going from bad to worse. Hattie was at the end of her tether but could not bring herself to come out into the open about her relationship with Steve. By now I was aware of the situation, Bruce having taken me into his confidence. I had given up my night-time job at the Establishment as I had been put in charge of the complaints department at work, for which I needed all my wits about me. It was a relief to have my evenings free again; it meant I could give more time to John, who was getting desperate. He broke down in tears one evening, but couldn't bring himself to voice his fears.

Then, at a party one evening, Hattie and Steve took me to one side and tried to explain how they saw the situation. Later Steve told me bluntly that John was mine for the taking. He even told me that I should have a very comfortable life if I married John, and ended up by saying that it would make them both very happy if I took John off their hands.

I found what Steve said very offensive and told him flatly that I thought it was tasteless to talk of palming John off in that way. As far as I was concerned he was a friend, but no more than that. Also he was a lot older than I was.

From that moment I took a dislike to Steve – how I wished that Hattie would come to her senses and get rid of him.

That summer I spent my holidays in Ramsgate as usual. It was during that time – on David's seventh birthday, in fact – that something happened that put my relationship with John on a different footing. It was a beautiful summer's day, so I decided to hold David's birthday party on the West Cliff beach. Beau was also in Ramsgate on holiday, and she and I packed a picnic and, accompanied by David and a bunch of his friends, we set off for the seaside. We were right in the thick of it, running races and having a competition to see who could build the best sandcastle, when John suddenly appeared. This surprised me for two reasons: first, John never turned up unexpectedly; second, he never went to the beach.

To say he was depressed was an understatement. He had come from Folkestone, where he had been filming *Those Magnificent Men in Their Flying Machines* with Tony Hancock, and the two of them had been commiserating with each other. Both were having marital problems, Tony was worried about his health, and together they had been knocking back quite a bit of booze.

To cheer himself up he took Beau and me out on the town that evening. We had a very merry time, ending up in a late-night drinking club, where John was collared by a fan. While they were talking I found myself looking at John dispassionately. For the first time it struck me how attractive he was, with his broad shoulders and fine, aristocratic features. At that moment he looked round and caught my eye. A little dart of desire hit me in the stomach.

'You do know that John is potty about you, don't you?' said Beau, ever quick to notice these things.

It was the first time I had thought about him other than as a dear, fatherly friend.

We drove home from the club and dropped Beau at her digs in London Road. As we waited for her to find her way down the drive to the front door John put his hand on my shoulder. He had often done this before, but this time it was different. He kissed me for the first time, and it was so exciting that we ended up making love in the car in a cul-de-sac round the corner from London Road. Nothing was said between us and later, when he left me at the door, I was in a state of total confusion. I had known him for less than eighteen months and the suddenness of this new state of affairs had knocked the ground from under me.

Seven

The realization that John and I had become lovers precipitated Hattie's urgency to bring matters to a head. Steve moved in with her, and John, although he had had his own room for some time, was now provided with a bed-sitting room in the house where he could live a more or less self-contained existence.

The fact that he had the comfort of my bed and body, however, made him no more secure. He didn't want to leave the home he had shared with Hattie for fourteen years or forego the pleasure of being near his sons, any more than I wanted to make any change in the status quo. I wasn't in love with John. I enjoyed having sex with him – in fact, sex with John was more abandoned and uninhibited than with anyone I'd ever known – but I wanted my life to continue just as it was. The human dilemma, how reluctant are we all to let go of things.

One night in a restaurant appropriately called Grumbles John proposed, although I didn't realize it was a proposal at the time. It came out in the middle of the conversation we were having about what he would do if he had to leave Eardley Crescent, their home in Earls Court. 'I have no idea where to go. I'm sure you don't want to take me on,' he said. That was a proposal of marriage. I let the whole thing pass over my head because no, I didn't want to take him on.

He went to Bognor Regis for a few weeks to work on *The Punch and Judy Man*, another film with Tony Hancock, and when he came back to London he decided to take himself off on a holiday to Tangier to try and sort things out. He was feeling tired and run down – the whole business was getting on top of him.

He had only been gone a day or so when Hattie rang me. He was in hospital in Gibraltar, having collapsed on a plane from Tangier. Almost immediately upon his arrival in Tangier he had fallen ill. He had managed to get on a plane for home but the stewardess, seeing how ill he was, arranged to have an ambulance waiting for him in Gibraltar and had personally accompanied him to the hospital. He had a collapsed lung, hepatitis and pneumonia; also, and much worse, there was a growth in his colon. He was so ill that the doctors gave him only a few hours to live and Hattie had been sent for urgently. Miraculously he pulled through. It was while I waited for news of his recovery that I realized how much he meant to me.

After about six weeks John came home looking gaunt and ill. Almost immediately he was admitted to hospital for an operation. Hattie was wonderful: she kept me informed of his progress and after the operation I was the first to be told that it had been a success. I visited him in hospital regularly and later spent a lot of time at Eardley Crescent keeping him company. However, his brush with death hadn't altered anything so far as Hattie's relationship was concerned: Steve was still there and she was as much in love as ever.

John and I were now what can only be described as going steady. Up to now our relationship had been on a more casual basis, particularly in public, but now he was spending more and more time in St George's Square and would come with me to Ramsgate at the weekends. He was talking of getting a flat of his own and asked me to live with him. I begged for more time and urged him to try living on his own for a time to see how he got along. 'Why don't you try living like a bachelor for a while?' I suggested. 'You might find that you enjoy it.' It was a vain hope. When it came to looking after himself, he was one of the most helpless people I have ever met. He didn't know one end of a tin opener from the other. I felt deep down that he was my responsibility, or would be before long, but though I cared for him I was still trying to hang on to my independence.

Come October 1964 we were spending every weekend together, and on one of them he took me to Lingfield to meet Tony Hancock. He was anxious for us to meet. He was proud to be one of Tony's closest and oldest friends and worried about him constantly.

Every time John returned from visiting Tony in some nursing home or other, where he was recovering from one of his periodic breakdowns, he would relate details of his visit with tears in his eyes. 'He was sitting dejectedly in the garden,' he told me once, 'trying to make a fucking coffee table in order to please his therapist.' The mental picture that this conjured up seemed like Tony at his most Hancockian and I had to smile to myself. But in general I imagined Tony to be an intense, self-involved hypochondriac, lacking the humour in real life that he so brilliantly displayed on the screen. To be honest, I wasn't too keen to meet him.

Imagine my surprise when he opened the front door to find this laughing expansive man with bright blue eyes, who swept me into his arms with a great welcoming hug. I was bowled over by him. Most celebrities seemed quite ordinary in the flesh. Not Tony. He was much larger than life, and certainly more attractive than I'd imagined him to be. I knew instantly why John was so fond of him.

'Welcome to MacKonkies,' he said, throwing his arm around John's shoulder affectionately. 'Come and meet Cis.' I shook hands with Cicely, his pretty blonde wife. She was friendly enough to us, but she had an air of remoteness about her in contrast to her husband.

We passed a pleasant day with them. I was flattered by how attentive Tony was, especially as John had told me that he was often ill at ease with women. At one point during the afternoon he took my hand and led me round the house and gardens, introducing me to his giant poodles, Charlie and Mr Brown. He fired all sorts of questions at me – What did I think about this piece of music? Had I read this book? and so on – and once, when I was sitting on the rug and I said something that made him laugh, he rolled backwards, lying helplessly on the floor with tears running down his face. I had never seen someone give himself up to mirth the way Tony did. I was fascinated by him.

Cicely drove us all to a local pub in the evening where we played shoveha'penny, and she and Tony insisted that we have dinner with them and stay the night. Over dinner Tony said to John, 'You've got to keep this one, Johnny,' nodding at me.

'I've asked her to marry me but she doesn't want to,' said John.

'Then you're a fool,' said Tony.

'I don't remember you asking me before,' I said, and changed the subject.

Just before the Christmas of 1964 John found a suitable flat in Barons Court. (To be honest, Hattie found it for him). He took me to see it. There was a bar and restaurant on the ground floor of the block, which would be handy for someone as helpless about food as John was.

He moved in the week before Christmas. On moving day I went straight from work to help him unpack. Dear John, the flat was in a hopeless muddle – he had put everything in the wrong place. It touched me to see his helplessness; I knew then I would have to care for him. By the time I'd rearranged things it looked more like a home, and I could see all sorts of things that could be done to make it look even better. He took me to dinner in Kensington and, over an extravagant and boozy meal, he proposed properly and I accepted.

That night I slept with him in the new flat, and the next morning he begged me to give up my job and move in right away. I found that giving up work was a bigger wrench than I had imagined, not for the work itself, but because it represented the last bastion of my independence and freedom. After the novelty of having nothing to do all day except clean the tiny flat and cook for John had worn off, I began to miss the ritual of dressing up for work and the company of the girls. I burst into tears one night when I was round at Beau's. More than anyone, Beau understood the importance of working and she urged me to get another job. But it was the one thing that John didn't want me to do, and I eventually settled my mind to being a lady of leisure.

However, there was one great advantage of not being tied to a job, and that was there were no more Sunday evening partings. When John was away I could spend all my spare time with David. We had discussed the possibility of having him to live with us in London but, in spite of missing me, he was happy in Ramsgate. He loved his school and had lots of friends. Besides which, my parents would have missed him and they argued that Ramsgate was a healthier place to bring up a child than London. So we left things as they were for the time being and I threw myself into the job of looking after John.

John was a darling to live with. He gave me the freedom to be myself and never tried to change me in any way. Indeed, he turned his life and his affairs over to me lock, stock and barrel. When he left Hattie he had £200, some furniture that she had sorted out for him, and the car. The Eardley Crescent house belonged to her and her mother, and she had little money of her own as she spent freely and extravagantly on her charity work and her friends. The £200 was put into a joint account. I was given a cheque book, Hattie taught me how to keep an account ledger, and from then on John never looked at a bank statement or knew how much money he had. He simply wanted to get on with his work and leave all those tasks to me. With Hattie's help I opened charge accounts at Derry and Tom's, Barkers and a wine merchant's. I had only to pick up the phone and everything was delivered.

A bigger flat became vacant next door to ours, and we took it over. It had large sunny rooms and a balcony, where I planted out windowboxes full of petunias and geraniums. We acquired a cleaner called Lynn, a dear old-fashioned soul who used to get all her words wrong and say things like 'congratulated iron' and 'creased lightning'. Once, when we bought a picture of the Crucifixion, she looked at it for a long time and then said, 'Wasn't that a shame.'

John was anxious to get married, and we arranged to let Hattie take proceedings against us, naming me as co-respondent, while I divorced Mark on the grounds of his desertion. It seemed the best way to go about things. It was all very amicable, although it entailed a visit from a private detective, who had to look into our bedroom to ensure that we really were living in sin. He kept clearing his throat in embarrassment when he asked us personal questions, much to our amusement.

Hattie divorced John and I divorced Mark on the same day. It was arranged between our solicitors that Hattie's case was heard first, and I was allowed to stand at the back of the courtroom while the divorce was being granted. Obviously in the eyes of the law we were supposed to be antagonists so we couldn't smile or acknowledge each other in any way, but as she left the room she blew me a kiss. It was summer 1965.

We were both on the front page of the *Evening Standard* that night. Under my photo the caption said, 'The other woman'. I wish the press could have seen us all celebrating later.

John and I married at Fulham Town Hall on 2 March 1966. Bruce was our best man. The wedding reception was held at the restaurant where John had finally proposed properly. Hattie sent us a lovely letter, which I still have, and Robin and Kim sent us a drawing of two goldfish with our names on them, swimming around in a bowl with two smaller fish with their names on them and heart-shaped bubbles.

At 6.30 the next morning we boarded a train for Manchester, where John was working at Granada with Warren Mitchell on a Comedy Half Hour series. Warren had just received the first script of *Till Death Us Do Part* and he regaled us all the way there with extracts from the script and a description of Alf Garnett. He was very funny, but we both had shocking champagne hangovers. We stayed in the same hotel as Warren, in the next room in fact. He was learning the clarinet at the time and would have a practice session every morning before leaving for the studios. John, who was very quiet in the mornings, to the point of silence, would greet him with, 'How nice to see you, Warren, much nicer than hearing you.'

While I was in Manchester I made a nostalgic visit. I took a taxi all the way to Oldham to visit my aunts, who were still living in the same houses in the same streets as they had all those years ago. We had been given a magnum of champagne as a wedding gift and I took it with me as an offering. When Aunt Dorothy opened her door to my knock it took quite some time for the penny to drop, as she hadn't seen me for some years. When it did, she clapped her hands together. 'Ee 'eck,' she shouted, 'it's our Joan.' Suddenly the street was full of aunts and cousins, all running from door to door shouting, 'Our Joan's come up to see us.' My grandparents' house hadn't changed at all except for the earth closet – there was a new flush toilet which they were very proud of. The front parlour was exactly the same. It was like going back in time to the days when, as a little girl, I would sit on that same sofa and escape with *Bunty of the Upper Fourth*, my hands calloused from Miss Bridget's cane. If only that little girl could have known that one day far in the future everything was going to be all right.

I went to Middleton Road. Our old house was still there, now a smart baker's shop. I looked up at the window of the room where Grandma had died and said a little prayer to her. Then I went to see the Lyric, but it had gone. A modern block of flats stood in its place. Later I took the family out for lunch at the best restaurant I could find and got them all tight. When I left them later that day, with passes for the recording of the show at the end of the week, I felt as though I had exorcised a ghost from the past. I've never been back to Oldham. My aunts and uncles are all dead and my cousins are all grandmothers like me.

During the months that John and I had been settling in together and putting down roots I had seen Tony on two occasions. The first time was at the Talk of the Town, where he was appearing in cabaret. He was looking tired and tense but seemed genuinely glad to see us. I met his mother Lily and his publicity agent Freddie Ross, who only let us stay for a few minutes before ushering us out.

The second time was when Tony was hosting *Sunday Night at the London Palladium*. Things were going badly for him: he had received bad reviews of the show and his private life was in chaos. We found him alone on this occasion, wrapped in a white towelling robe. He looked grey and puffy, and his hands were shaking. 'Well,' I said, 'if this is what show business does, I'd rather be a lavatory attendant,' and he laughed ruefully.

By then his marriage to Cicely had ended and he had married Freddie Ross, an efficient career woman who had been his publicity agent for fourteen years and upon whom he had come to depend. Their brief marriage was peppered with drama. Tony was drinking heavily and was in and out of nursing homes, where he was dried out, relieved of vast amounts of money, filled with tranquillizers and sent home none the better. Alcohol was his cloak of comfort, his retreat from reality, and he couldn't or wouldn't give it up. His marriage to Freddie only lasted six months and the downward spiral continued.

We read in the papers that Freddie had taken an overdose of sleeping pills, and that Tony had gone off to Blackpool leaving her in a coma. Then we heard that he had walked out of the show. John tried to make contact with him, but he had gone into hiding and couldn't be found.

The summer of 1966 was long and hot and much of my time was spent in Ramsgate. Kim came to stay with us, John joined us at the weekends, and the boys and I would spend long days on the beach. Dorothy Squires, who was an old friend, had invited the two boys to spend the last week of their summer holidays at her home in Bexley and at the end of the week John and I drove down to pick them up. They were in the swimming pool when we arrived, and we watched them desperately gleaning the last moments of the day. The autumn term was looming and a faint air of melancholy that often comes in late August seemed to waft across the garden. As we left I remember looking back and feeling an ominous shiver.

We drove to London, dropped Kim at Hattie's and settled David into bed, and just as we were finishing dinner the telephone rang. It was Tony, and from that day on my life was to take a violent and unexpected turn.

Joan Le Mesurier outside her home in Sitges, Spain

Grandma with Dad (right) and Uncle Harry in Ramsgate, 1910

Mum (looking like Bebe Daniels) and her parents at Folkestone, 1939

Mum and Dad on the prom
around 1945

Bridget with Joan and
brothers David and
Terry, about 1938

First marriage to Mark Eden, 1953

Joan's son, David Malin

Emma and Joan in the park, 1984

John Le Mesurier

Above: Tony once said to me that it was years before he had the
courage to walk onto a stage without a hat.

Opposite: the 'two faces' of Hanc

John and Joan in
Ramsgate, 1964

John and Joan with
Nicodemus, Ramsgate,
1981

Eight

Tony Hancock was a living legend. For fifteen years he reigned as the undisputed king of British comedy. It was said that on Friday nights when his radio programme *Hancock's Half Hour* was on the air, and later the television series, the pubs and fish and chip shops suffered because people stayed in. He had the distinction of being called by his surname, and he inspired such love in his public that they felt they owned a part of him, and greeted him as a long-lost friend. To this day, twenty years after his death, he remains a cult figure. A one-man show, *Hancock's Last Half Hour*, has been performed all over the world.

When the Festival Hall had a season of Hancock's work recently, it sold out before the first night. My son, David, went to the last show, and at the end of the evening the audience was on its feet and cheering Tony as though he were present.

I haven't written here about his work, only about my relationship with him, but many excellent books have been written about his career; one by Philip Oakes captures the lovable and exasperating nature of the man and describes the problems of trying to work with such a complex talent.

His second wife, Freddie Hancock, who spent fifteen years as his publicity agent before their marriage, has also written an excellent book which covers his professional life in great detail, and I would recommend it to any Hancock fan.

I can only write of my short time with him. I only wanted the man, but unfortunately the legend came too.

*

Tony had been hiding in his flat in Knightsbridge. After Freddie had left him he had removed all traces of her from his life. All her furniture and possessions had gone, and he had stayed alone, not answering the phone or the door, steeped in melancholy and alcohol. Finally, unable to bear his self-imposed exile any longer, he rang John and asked for help. Delighted to be of service, John went to get him and found him sitting on the floor surrounded by empty bottles. When Tony walked through our door grinning inanely, I was shocked how ill and thin he looked. This time I gave him a welcoming hug, happy to have the chance of mothering him. I had prepared some food but he wasn't hungry; he just wanted to drink, and talk, but not about himself. He neatly evaded the subject. He just wanted companionship. I put the food in front of him and managed to get the odd spoonful down him from time to time, like coaxing a child. That night, drunk and defeated as he was, he was still wonderful company, and we sat up until the small hours, when, in spite of his reluctance, I made up a bed for him on the couch, gave him a robe, and forced him to get undressed and go to sleep.

The following morning I came into the dining room to find David and Tony deep in conversation at the breakfast table. David had shown Tony where everything was and, to my amazement, they had made tea and toast. Tony had clearly scored a hit with my son. If David didn't like people, he would be polite but quiet, but with Tony he was talking animatedly. He enjoyed Tony's company so much, he was reluctant to go back to school.

Tony stayed with us for a week. He never dressed or left the flat, but ambled round in John's dressing gown, content to be in the company of friends. We didn't leave him alone. If I went to the shops, John stayed with him, and if John went out, I stayed in. I cooked extravagant dinners, and, although he was drinking more than was good for him, he began to eat and his appetite grew. While John was learning his lines Tony would sit in the kitchen and talk to me as I prepared dinner, following about like an amiable bloodhound, asking questions, but saying nothing about his marriage or his problems. I too enjoyed his company: although in some ways he could be a demanding guest, he was stimulating and amusing. He never flirted with me – the idea of Hancock flirting with anyone would have seemed ridiculous. I didn't realize at the time, but the feeling growing between us was much more serious.

On the following Monday John began work on a David Niven film called *Where the Spies Are*. After he had left for the studio, Tony said, 'Did you know that I'm an alcoholic?' It was a rare moment of honesty about his condition.

I replied that I had suspected as much.

'I've got to do a week in Eastbourne, starting next Monday. It's a tryout of some new material for a one-man show I'm doing at the Festival Hall at the end of the month and Delfont's have booked me into a rest home for a week to dry out. I've promised to go in today. Will you come with me?'

I felt a twist of disappointment at the thought of losing his company, but I was flattered to be needed.

Later that day Tony rang for his car. I laughed when I saw it parked outside the building. 'My God,' I said, 'that's modest.' It was a huge Cadillac, silver-blue with all the trimmings and a uniformed chauffeur. It didn't seem to fit the image of the man I had come to know.

On the way to the nursing home in Highgate we didn't say much, but Tony held my hand all the way like a child being taken to the dentist, and I felt a similar reluctance at handing him over.

When we arrived we were shown into an emergency room full of oxygen cylinders and medical paraphernalia. While we were waiting for his psychiatrist a nurse brought us tea and biscuits. I was eager to be gone – I felt that I had no right to be there – but Tony insisted that I stay and see him settled in. Over tea he said, 'How romantic, our first meal alone together.'

When the psychiatrist arrived, I again tried to leave, but

Tony held on to my hand. 'Mrs Le Mesurier is a close friend. You can speak freely,' he said, and I had to sit there while the man read the riot act to him as if he were a naughty schoolboy. I was embarrassed, but the lecture seemed to go over Tony's head. At last, still protesting, he was led away to his room. Before he went he made me promise that John and I would visit him that night. This we did, only to be told when we arrived that he was under sedation.

When we got home the flat seemed empty without him.

The Delfont Agency rang me the next afternoon. Tony wanted to know if I would meet him at the Prince of Wales Theatre at eleven o'clock that night. He would be rehearsing there after the theatre had closed to the public. It was an odd request, but he needed moral support. I went, with John's blessing.

I sat in the vast empty theatre while Tony and his accompanist, Kenny Clayton, went through his act. Tony was walking about disconsolately and after about fifteen minutes he had had enough. He took me to the Talk of the Town, where we sat in a corner of the bar, drank coffee and held hands, until it was time for him to go back to Highgate. The same routine happened every night that week. A taxi would pick me up at about 10.30 and drop me back home late that night. The light had gone out of Tony during those meetings; the sedatives had dulled him and he was vague and slightly dreamy, without his confidence-restoring alcohol.

At the end of the week Tony left for Eastbourne and John and I settled back into our comfortable routine, though perhaps comfortable is the wrong word. The past two weeks had shaken me up and left me feeling restless and excited. The following week John was told he was needed in Paris to do some location shots for the film. Instead of going to Ramsgate, I arranged to stay in London that weekend in order to see him off on the Saturday evening.

On the Saturday night I went out with Marion and

Dinny, who by this time had rented a flat close by in Barons Court. During the evening Dinny asked me if I was seeing anyone else. 'Whatever gave you that idea?' I asked him indignantly. He replied that I seemed absent-minded, which in his experience was a sure sign of love, and that if I wasn't having an affair I was certainly in the mood for one. As it turned out, it was a very astute observation.

On the Sunday I was having a lie-in when the phone rang. It was Tony in Eastbourne.

'Could you and John put me up for a few days?' he said. 'I can't face going back to the flat just yet.'

My heart missed a beat.

'Tony, I'd love to, but John isn't here. He's gone to Paris, and I was planning to go down to Ramsgate next week,' I lied.

'Look,' he said, 'I'll be out all day. I'm rehearsing for this show and it's scaring the shit out of me. I'm sure John won't mind.'

I agreed to let him stay that night, and promised to arrange for our cleaning lady to come during the week to look after him while I was away. I tried to make it clear to him that I had to go to Ramsgate.

I was having some friends over for lunch that same day, so I told Tony that if he didn't want to see anybody he should not arrive too early. 'OK, I'll be there this evening,' he said, and hung up. However, to the surprise and delight of my guests, he turned up during lunch and the whole occasion developed into a party. He was at his best that day, in the company of my friends, all of whom were actors. Needless to say, they were also Hancock fans. Everyone, including me, drank more than usual and the party went on into the evening.

While I was making coffee in the kitchen Tony joined me. 'I've missed you,' he said and put his arm round me.

That was the moment when I should have used all my control and stopped things from going any further. But I didn't. What I said was, 'Please don't go on with this because I can't fight you.'

That was all he needed. Within minutes he had got rid of my guests and we were alone. We sat at the table and he poured us a drink. The energy between us was so immense that we were both shaking.

'I'm John's best friend and I'm in love with his wife,' he said. 'I'm sorry, I didn't intend this to happen.' I'm sure that he meant what he said. 'What are we going to do?'

'Let's sleep on it,' I said.

By the next morning I had promised to leave John and marry Tony. Our lovemaking, as close and fulfilling as our companionship, had stripped away the last vestige of control. We were in the grip of what can only be described as a grand passion. In one single night Tony had become the centre of my life and his happiness my first priority.

During those first few days nothing was allowed to interfere with the mutual delight we felt in each other's company. I told Lynn, my cleaning lady, that I could manage without her for the week, we took the phone off the hook and we stayed alone, talking, making love and getting to know everything about each other. At night we would ring for a taxi and go out to dinner to a quiet restaurant, finding it exciting that we had a secret nobody else knew about.

One morning a card arrived from John. 'Here I am in Paris, France. Can't wait to get home to my little friend and wife,' it said. The reality of what had happened made my stomach churn. I told Tony I couldn't leave John; we would have to keep our relationship secret and see each other when we could.

But Tony wouldn't hear of it. 'It wouldn't be honest,' he said. 'We wouldn't be able to hide our feelings. It would make John more unhappy in the long run.' He offered to tell John for me, but I couldn't have let him do that. I begged him for more time, but he wanted it done as soon as John came back.

I needed a friend to talk to, so I rang Marion and asked her to come over. Tony bowled her over with the strength of his feelings. By the end of the evening she was on his side, agreeing that it was better to make a clean break, but I kept thinking about John's gentleness and his love for Tony. I felt as if I were about to commit a murder.

Tony rang his mother and broke the news to her. He made me speak to her on the phone. She was on his side as well. No one doubted the sincerity of our feelings for each other. Indeed, I had no qualms on that score, not then nor in the time to come. It seemed right and natural to be with Tony, as if we had always been together. But in spite of his bravado, Tony was as horrified at the thought of hurting John as I was; yet he was equally horrified at the thought of losing me. By convincing others, he was trying to convince himself that he was right. He pulled out every stop and in the end John's fate was sealed.

Tony wanted to be with me when I confronted John, but I knew John wouldn't be able to bear that. The intensity of our emotions would have mortified him. It was something I had to do in private. To this day I go cold at the thought of it. I loved them both; I could have lived with and cared for both of them – anything but cause such pain to someone as undeserving of it as John.

John was due back on the Saturday. On the Friday Tony, unable to face the silence of his flat, checked in to the Mayfair Hotel and took the Maharajah Suite. At moments of insecurity he was given to making grandiose gestures. I agreed to have dinner with him that evening at the hotel. Just before I left the flat Beau rang and I asked her to meet me in the hotel bar. I needed her common-sense approach; I also needed her friendship – inside I felt like a child who had done something wrong.

I told her what had happened. 'My God, whatever are you thinking of?' was her reaction. She was shocked and deeply sorry for John. I asked her to come upstairs and meet Tony. 'You mean he's here, in the hotel?' she said, her blue eyes wide with surprise. 'I don't think I should. It seems so disloyal to John.' But I wanted her to meet Tony so that she would understand how I felt, and in the end she agreed to come.

The opulence of the suite overwhelmed us both. It even had a kitchen and a terrace.

'I don't see you for three weeks, and this is what happens,' said Beau. 'It's certainly not boring having a friend like you.'

Tony asked her to stay and have dinner with us. We both were feeling uneasy about the coming day and her down-to-earth humour was a comfort to us both.

As she left, Tony rang the desk. 'Would you have a taxi waiting for Lady Newton,' he said, 'and put in on my bill.'

After Beau had gone I stayed with Tony for a while. He wanted me to stay the night but, frightened as I was, I had to face the night alone. I needed that last bit of solitude to think clearly about the consequences of what I was doing. But even in the short time I had known Tony, without him there I felt as if a piece of myself were missing. Whatever happened, I was unable to give him up.

I made Marion come with me to the airport to meet John. I needed her there for moral support, but as soon as she saw him ambling towards us she changed her mind. 'You can't do it,' she said. But something had hardened inside me and I knew that I would.

John gave a sigh of relief when we arrived at the apartment. He had bought French perfume for us both and he invited Marion out to dinner with us to celebrate his homecoming. In the restaurant he asked me if I had heard from Tony, I answered briefly that he was getting ready for the Festival Hall concert and then changed the subject. When John left the table Marion again begged me not to go through with it. Her fondness for John has overridden the certainty she had felt in Tony's presence.

Unable to bear the suspense a moment longer, I cut the evening short by saying that I was tired. We dropped Marion off at her flat. The moment of truth had arrived.

I told John what had happened as soon as we got indoors. He tried to understand. 'If it had been anyone else, I wouldn't –' he said. Even then he didn't get angry – it would have been so much easier if he had. He just walked up and down hugging himself, and then he wept. I couldn't bear it, and, having plunged the knife in, I tried to withdraw it. I told him it was pity I felt for Tony, and that as soon as he was back on his feet I would return. I was shocked at my cruelty – it was the hardest thing I have ever done. I gave John a sleeping pill and got him into bed, and spent a tearful and sleepless night.

Early the next morning I rang Tony. He also had spent a terrible night. When I told him how awful it had been he begged me to let him come over and share it with me. 'Anything is better than this,' he said. But I couldn't bear to put John through any more distressing scenes.

Later that day I asked Marion to come over and stay with John – I couldn't bear the thought of leaving him on his own. Then I left to join Tony.

When I arrived at the Mayfair Tony was talking to John on the telephone. He had been drinking and was weeping. He passed the phone to me. 'I want you to know that we are not happy about this situation,' I said.

John ended up consoling me. What an absurd mess it all was.

'I can't do it to him after all. You've got to go back to him,' Tony said, and we both cried in each other's arms. I told Tony that, to soften the blow, I had promised John that I would go back when Tony had done the Festival Hall concert. When we had composed ourselves we decided to concentrate all our energies on getting him fit for it and making sure he was word perfect; afterwards we would review the situation. It made us feel less guilty about what we had done and gave us breathing space in which to be together.

That evening John's doctor, who had been called in by Marion, rang me at the hotel and asked if he could talk to me alone. We arranged to meet in the bar.

He began by telling me what I was putting John through, as if I was unaware of it, and then explained what living with an alcoholic would involve. 'He's too far gone,' he said. 'He will drag you down with him.'

In my ignorance I swept aside his warnings. 'He drinks because he's unsure of himself. He needs care, affection and security. I can give him those things,' I told him, confident of the power of love.

The doctor was a kind man. He had looked after Hattie and John for years. He knew about Hattie's lover and was appalled that John should be betrayed all over again by me. But he saw that it was hopeless trying to change my mind. At least he had discharged his duty so far as John was concerned. He kissed me, wished me luck and departed.

I recounted the conversation to Tony, who vowed that he would keep his drinking to a minimum. He agreed that with me beside him to help and support him, there would be no need for alcohol, and he promised that every evening he would study his lines with me. At that time I had no idea what living with an alcoholic was like. I knew nothing of the lies and the self-deception I would have to deal with. But even if I had known I would still have been unable to leave him. It was fate to learn what love, real love, was truly like. It wasn't pretty or romantic, but a hard, gruelling lesson, in which I would be tested time and time again.

The next morning Tony's mother arrived unexpectedly. We were making love on the floor of the bathroom at the time. 'Are you in there, Tony?' she called, knocking on the door.

I was deeply embarrassed and tried to scramble to my feet, but Tony, who enjoyed this sort of situation, refused to let me up. A silent struggle followed, with me getting more and more ruffled at the idea of what his mother would think, until Tony called out, 'All right, Lily, we're just coming,' and then went off into fits of laughter.

'You can be so vulgar sometimes,' I hissed at him. 'That's your mother out there.'

This only made him worse. 'You don't know Lily,' he said, wiping his eyes.

When we finally emerged, wearing the his and hers bathrobes provided by the hotel, Lily was in the living room ordering tea. Tony introduced me to her, although I had met her fleetingly two years before, in his dressing room at the Talk of the Town.

Tony was laughing and benevolent, glad to have her support and approval and proud to introduce us. He had a very close relationship with her. She had an amazing knowledge and love of sport – they would go on at great length about golf and cricket, arguing over points and scores like a couple of men friends. Over lunch that day I sat spellbound while she related stories about the family and Tony's childhood.

'She never let me grow up,' he said. 'Once we were out on a drive and she said to me, "Look at the choo-choo puff-puff".'

'Well, what's wrong with that ?' I said.

'I was thirty-two at the time.'

She was a great laugher, like Tony. In the past, when the family were all together they were always laughing. His brother Roger would try to climb up the wall. Tony would roll on his back and wave his legs in the air, and the eldest brother, Colin, would kneel on all fours, banging his fists on the ground, all of them fighting for breath. Lily had been married four times, all her husbands had died. Colin had been killed in the war, shot down during a bombing raid. Tony's father had died of cancer. He must have been an amazing man. Even in the last stages of his illness, when he was terribly emaciated, he would wrap a sheet around himself and give impersonations of Gandhi.

One of Lily's husbands had been in the business. Lily had been his accompanist. In those days variety artists would take the same act out on the road for year after year without changing a word. Lily had seen the act hundreds of times, yet she never failed to laugh at every joke. The ending was a monologue about a little dog and a lonely old man, and she would sit at the piano mopping her eyes and shaking with tears.

It was easy to see where Tony's humour came from. Lily and he were like a double act. She was quite delicate and would describe her health problems as being something wrong 'down below'.

Tony would roar with laughter. 'Get your legs round a good man,' he would say. 'That'll put you right,' and she would raise her eyes to the ceiling in refined despair.

It was lovely having her near – she made everything seem normal. While Tony was rehearsing we would go for walks in Green Park. She would hold on to my arm and tell me about Tony's childhood. She had hoped that he would have academic leanings and had sent him to Bradfield College, but at sixteen he had flatly refused to stay on. One visiting day she had gone to the Dean's office to discuss his progress, which, apart from his interest in cricket, was nil. At the end of the meeting the Dean told her that she would find Tony leaving the hall with the rest of his class.

'How will I pick him out of that mob?' she said.

'It's simple,' the Dean replied dryly. 'He'll be the only one with his mortar board stuffed under his arm and his gown trailing on the ground.'

I went to see John every day. He was bearing up. The word had got about and friends had rallied round. His air of helplessness always brought people scurrying to his aid. It was a relief to know that he wasn't alone.

In spite of our promises to him, after only a few days together Tony and I both knew that we would be unable to part after the show. Tony was busy making plans for our future. He was anxious for me to tell my parents. He wanted me to burn all my bridges so that there would be no going back and so that the commitment we had made to each other would be sealed by being out in the open.

I broke the news to them on the phone. They took it well, but of course it was a shock. My parents loved John and were delighted at how well our marriage had turned out. They had a gentleman for a son-in-law and they dropped his name outrageously. Dad felt protective towards John, who in turn admired my father's nature. Now John was being ousted by a man who, no matter how much my parents admired him on the screen, in real life meant nothing but trouble.

To my Dad's everlasting credit, he delivered no moral lectures. He said my life and who I spent it with were none of his business. Like John, he hated emotional showdowns and would go to any length to avoid them.

Then Tony took the phone from me and spoke to my father. He told him that we would really appreciate my parents' understanding, but even if that was not forthcoming we would still stay together. He said that his feeling for me was genuine and promised my father that I would be loved and protected.

After breaking the ice, Tony was in a fever to meet them. He was elated at their acceptance of him. It was a great victory – another bond had been forged, a fusing with my family, and he had to meet them right away. The fact that the show was looming ever closer was of secondary importance. Tony insisted on taking a night off: we would drive down to Ramsgate and stay overnight in a hotel, and go and see my parents.

The following morning when we were due to leave for Ramsgate Tony asked for the car to be waiting outside the hotel. As it was a fine day, he ordered the driver to have the hood down and the radio playing. He was swaggering, at his most Hancockian, and I felt hot with embarrassment. 'I hate this bloody car,' I said as we drove away. 'I think it's vulgar. If anyone who knows me were to see me, they'd think I'd left John for all the wrong reasons.'

Tapping the ash from his cigarette, Tony said to the driver, 'Sell the car and get a Mercedes.'

'Certainly, Mr Hancock,' said the driver.

And off we went to meet my apprehensive parents.

Nine

The journey to Ramsgate was punctuated by several refreshment breaks, then a great burst of speed well above the permitted limit when we reached the motorway. The hood of the Cadillac was still down and the wind played havoc with my hair and my carefully applied mascara started to run. I ended up looking like a rather disgruntled panda. As we left the motorway Tony asked the driver to put up the hood so that I could tidy myself. The driver slowed the car to a crawl and, at the touch of a button, the hood began to rise over the gleaming flashy convertible. A gang of motorcyclists were having a smoke by the roadside and they began to jeer and catcall at this phenomenon, but as soon as they recognized Tony their derision turned to applause and admiring whistles. Tony, flushed by the speed and the alcohol, stood up in the back of the car and waved regally as the hood began to descend, and we passed grandly on.

We had reserved a room at a discreet hotel situated on the cliffs between Broadstairs and Ramsgate and we went there first to freshen up and leave our luggage. At my request, Tony sent the car and driver back to London. I was nervous enough at the prospect of the coming meeting without the added embarrassment of being seen cruising around the streets of Ramsgate in a large blue limousine with my new lover.

We arrived by taxi at my parents' house. Mother was there with her two sisters, my aunts Mildred and Dorothy, who were on a rare visit from Oldham. The three of them had worked themselves up into a state of twittering anxiety by the time we appeared. Dad was out, walking around his beloved harbour. He was dreading the coming confrontation with Tony and was attempting to compose himself in the face of this new and unwanted intrusion into the order and tranquillity of his life.

Tony, eager to win their approval, had armed himself with several bottles of Dom Perignon champagne. On meeting my mother, he swept her into his arms with one of his great friendly hugs and then did the same to my overawed aunties. The champagne was produced and they were immediately put at ease by his warmth and humour. In no time at all he had them talking about themselves, reminiscing about their days spent working as weavers in a cotton mill. He roared with laughter at their anecdotes and quaint North Country expressions, and they, helped by the wine and the soft haze of retrospection, were transformed into three giggling girls.

Tony had a natural gift: he was a wonderful listener – it was what had helped to make him a star. He had a genuine curiosity about people from all walks of life and knew how to ask the right questions and how to draw them out without being patronizing. He never dominated a scene, being content to observe. By the time my father arrived home the ladies were completely captivated and Tony was one of the family.

As I had anticipated, Tony took to my father on sight. Everybody loved Dad – it was impossible not to. He and Tony had the same sense of humour. Dad was a naturally witty man, and in spite of his concern for John and the worry we were causing, Dad was totally bowled over by Tony's natural charm. I breathed a sigh of relief when, raising his glass, he said, 'Here's to you both. I can't pretend that I'm not unhappy about John. He's a good man and we think the world of him. But it's not my business to sit in judgement on you. You're both old enough to know what you feel about each other, so welcome to the family.

And Tony, visibly moved, put his arm round my

shoulder and said, 'I'll take good care of her, Fred, you can count on that.'

So we all had another glass of champagne and Tony and I went off to meet David from school.

Apart from David's embarrassment at finding Tony, quite unaware of the fact that he had been recognized, standing at the school gates amid a group of waiting mothers, with the gift of a football under his arm, the first visit was a success. Tony had no idea how to deal with children. He was shy in their company, as he was with most women. So his idea of giving David a good time was to rush him into an ice-cream parlour and talk about football while David forced down a huge Knickerbocker Glory. But David was already hooked, and in spite of all the horrors that were to come and my parents' eventual rejection of Tony, David remained steadfastly devoted.

We returned to London the following day with a sense of relief that we had at least broken the ice as far as my parents were concerned. In truth, we had only thrown them into a deeper state of confusion because now they felt a sense of disloyalty towards John, who visited them as often as he could, being in need of their support and affection.

Only one week was left until the dreaded Festival Hall performance and Tony could not, or would not, concentrate on rehearsing the new material that had been written for him. The only thing he wanted to rehearse was his farewell speech. The strongly self-destructive side of his nature was intrigued by the idea of 'going out with a bang and not a whimper', which was an expression that came all too readily to his lips. He also fantasized about 'dying on the job' when we were making love.

His favourite theatrical anecdote was the story of two elderly comics who had carried the same tired old act around the halls for years. They would stroll on to the stage wearing moth-eaten fur coats and deliver their lines lying on their stomachs, their chins in their hands as they rested on their elbows. One hot afternoon in a little theatre out in the sticks there were only twenty people in the audience. They went through their usual routine and, after receiving no applause or enthusiasm, they got to their feet and dusted themselves down. Then one of them said wearily, 'Ladies and gentlemen, my partner and I wish to thank you for your overwhelming ovation. So if you will kindly remain seated we will pass among you and beat the shit out of you with a baseball bat.'

But although Tony said that he was tired of the business and would talk wistfully about settling down with me, only a small facet of his nature would have been content to do that. His fame and his massive success had ruined him – they had prevented him from being 'ordinary'.

But I wasn't to know that all those years ago. I innocently believed that, after clearing the hurdle of his one-man show at the Festival Hall, he would thankfully rest for ever on his laurels and live happily with me in rural simplicity. How little I knew him! But I so desperately wanted his swan song to be a triumph that every day I would urge him to rehearse so that he would be word-perfect.

Among the new material he had to deliver a long speech from *King Lear* – 'Blow winds and crack your cheeks . . .'. I had gone through it so many times I could have said it backwards. In the middle of it Tony would say, 'How about this? "Ladies and gentlemen, as I'm obviously dying a death up here I'm not going to bore you any longer with this load of old rubbish, all of which you have heard before, so I'm off to Ramsgate to fuck my brains loose." Or "Ladies, gentlemen and Lily (his mother), owing to the fact that I have been fucked from arsehole to breakfast time of late, I have come to the conclusion that there's more to life than standing on a stage making a prick of myself."' Then he would throw his script over his shoulder and change the subject. He became so obsessed with the idea of burning all his bridges in this way that I began to believe he would really go through with it and my apprehension grew as the show loomed nearer.

Two nights before the show he woke me up in the small hours. He was sweating and shaking uncontrollably. He was suffering from a virulent attack of diarrhoea and was in a state of pure terror. 'I can't go through with it,' he kept repeating. 'What am I thinking of?' His lips were blue and his teeth chattering so violently that I thought he would have a heart attack. It took some time to calm him down, but after a couple of tranquillizers and a hot bath the shaking subsided and I got him back into bed and cuddled him.

'If you don't want to go on with this I'll understand,' he said with his head on my shoulder.

'Don't be daft' I replied, stroking his hair. In the ensuing silence I sang softly in his ear, 'There's no business like show business, like no business I know . . .'

'Everything about it is appalling,' he answered, and we giggled ourselves to sleep.

By the next morning he was in command of himself and the episode was never mentioned. I never saw that side of him again, but at the time it deepened my feeling for him, and I'll never forget it.

On the day of the show he was resigned and calm. He had decided to do his old act and, as a consolation and a buffer against the dread of the coming evening, he made plans for us to leave for Ramsgate the following morning. We were going to escape, to find a house with a garden for David and live happily ever after. On the phone to a journalist who asked what his future plans were, he said, 'I'm going to Ramsgate for the fishing.'

'Why Ramsgate?' asked the journalist.

'None of your business,' he answered in his Noël Coward voice.

At six o'clock that evening I went with him to the Festival Hall and left him at the stage door. We didn't speak on the way. We held hands, and I remembered the other journey I had made with him to the nursing home less than a month ago. I experienced the same feeling of reluctance at letting him go into his other life. As I watched him walk away, his shoulders hunched and his head thrust forward, he reminded me of a rather small brave bull going into the arena to meet his end.

At the door he looked over his shoulder. 'Do me a favour,' he said, smiling ruefully. 'Ring your dad and find out if there's a vacancy for a crane driver in Ramsgate. I'm going to be out of a job by tomorrow.' And then he was gone, and I went back to the hotel to get ready for the coming ordeal.

Lily and I had been given seats right at the back of the theatre, on the top level to keep us out of his eyeline and to enable us to make a fast getaway at the end of the show. I was shaking with nerves, much to Lily's amusement. 'He's going to be fine,' she said. 'If you had been through this as many times as I have you wouldn't worry.' But I couldn't be calmed. I just prayed for the show to be over so that I could go and get him and keep him safe. When the lights dimmed I felt as if I were about to witness a public execution, and when he walked on to the huge stage, looking so small in the vast space, I remembered him saying that the loneliest journey in the world was from the wings to the centre of the stage.

The audience, however, rose to their feet at his appearance and cheered him to a man. The waves of love that came over from them to him lifted him up and got him through. To be honest, if he had stood on his head and read the telephone directory, they would still have cheered him to the roof. It was pure nostalgia, a thank-you for his past glories. But that night it felt like a triumph, such was the emotion that this complex and talented man conjured up in his audience. Seen later on television the mistakes were obvious. His appearance, thin and emaciated as he was at that time, bore little resemblance to the Hancock of the past. And without the hysteria and warmth of a live audience it was a cold and bloodless piece of television.

But he got through it without the farewell speech and the quick getaway, though in a sense it *was* his farewell, to the BBC at least, as it was the last time he ever worked for them. However, on that night, after his standing ovation, during which for one moment he looked up to the back of the hall and made a gesture as if to plunge his hand down the front of his trousers, the sense of relief that I experienced was euphoric.

Leaving Lily in the care of the driver, I rushed backstage. Tony's dressing room was a sea of people. It was jammed with celebrities. Over their heads I caught sight of him, grey, sweating and trapped. When he saw me he mouthed, 'Get me out.' I fought my way to him, he reached out his hand, I grabbed it and rudely, without ceremony, pulled him away.

We ran for it. The moment we had longed for had arrived and we escaped, free at last to begin to live our own lives, or so I truly believed on that wonderful night.

Back at the Maharajah Suite, Lily, Tony and I celebrated. The switchboard was told no calls were to be put through and Tony ordered a delicious supper to be sent up – caviar, smoked salmon, Dom Perignon champagne – no expense spared. We were both suddenly ravenous, having been too tense and apprehensive to eat anything substantial for days. Over supper the three of us held a postmortem on the show, admitting our fears and roaring with relief. After Lily had left us to go to bed, Tony sent for more wine, and the two of us partied on into the small hours.

The next morning we were in a fever to get away. Lily left for Bournemouth by car, I packed, while Tony was occupied by numerous telephone calls from the press and his agents. As I was getting his things together I came across a pair of cufflinks engraved with the words 'If I had a talent like yours' on one and 'I'd be proud not scared' on the other. Tony, seeing me with them in my hand, snatched them from me. He turned to one of the maids who was cleaning up the breakfast things. 'Are you married?' he asked her. 'Yes,' she replied.

'Then give those to your husband. They might give him a bit of confidence.'

They were from Freddie. The gesture was typical of

Tony, ruthlessly sweeping out of his life everything from the past.

I was glad to be leaving the Mayfair. The opulence of the suite oppressed me. It seemed a vulgar way to be living, and so public. Waiters kept sidling in with trolleys and trays and maids kept cleaning up after us. There had been enough publicity about the collapse of Tony's marriage for them to know that I wasn't his wife. What must they have thought of me? These things mattered much more in those days than they do now and, in spite of our bravado, they mattered to us as well.

I wanted somewhere private where we could close our own door, where I could cook for Tony and clean up our own mess. I wanted somewhere tranquil, away from prying eyes, somewhere simple. Tony was only too ready to acquiesce. He alternated between extravagance and frugality with amazing speed, and our stay at the Mayfair had set him back a packet.

Before we left the hotel I asked him to tell the driver to keep the hood of the convertible up: I did not want us to make an exhibition of ourselves as on the previous occasion. But as we got to the swing doors Tony grabbed the collar of my coat and dragged me through them backwards. It was his idea of a joke, but it drew attention to us and I hated it.

'That's the second time you've made me feel like a whore when leaving this hotel,' I said when we were in the car. 'I never want to go there again.'

'Never mind, you parochial creature,' said Tony, roaring with laughter at my ruffled feathers. 'We'll find somewhere different.' And we certainly did.

It was a first-floor flat in a crumbling Victorian house on Ramsgate seafront. There was a 'To let' sign in the window and it was as distant from the Maharajah Suite at the Mayfair Hotel as one could imagine. A stunned landlady led us up to three rooms of such transcendental horror that we both gasped with delight. The kitchen floor was covered with curling red lino and contained (along with the obligatory cooker) one of those hideous green and cream enamel kitchen dressers with a pull-down worktop. There was a blue formica table under the window, flanked by two red plastic and chrome chairs. And there was a hook-on draining board attached to the sink. It was made of aluminium and was bent and crooked so that things were always sliding off. The floorboards were loose so that the whole kitchen jingled musically when we walked across it. The living room contained a brown plastic three-piece suite with red upholstered seats, a hideous sideboard, a worn, threadbare rug over more peeling linoleum, a hissing old gas fire with a coin meter alongside, and two cheap prints of sailing boats at peril on stormy seas.

It was £6 a week, expensive for a place like that, but it was a 'holiday flat', the landlady said, and she didn't usually let it out of season. She agreed to make an exception for us. So Tony paid her two weeks' in advance and it was ours. Our first home.

On our first night we sat up in bed laughing uncontrollably under a dangling, pink satin, fringed lampshade with an ingenious pull switch, admiring the curtains, which were orange and white polka dot with moth holes and which hung on a sagging white plastic cord.

It was a honeymoon period for us. There was no telephone and nobody except David and my parents knew where we were. We would pick David up from school and take him on the beach with the football or play in the public gardens in front of the flat. We would take him back to my parents at bedtime, and be content to be alone together in the evening with no other company save a transistor radio.

Tony's drinking was down to a minimum during that time. Everything was new and exciting between us and we needed nothing extraneous. We pushed all thoughts of John to the back of our minds and wallowed in our new-found joy. I don't believe any building has ever contained as much laughter or happiness as that flat. But it couldn't last. We couldn't stay there permanently. It was no place in which to put down roots or bring up a child, so we started to look around for something better.

We found it in Broadstairs. It was a modern bungalow, with a large living room, one wall of which was all windows looking out on the garden which ran down to the cliffs. It had four bedrooms and a big kitchen, central heating, and the telephone was already installed. The rent was £13 a week furnished, with an option to buy. And it was called Coq d'Or. It sported a weather vane in the shape of a cockerel and there were cock motifs on the iron gates. A bad omen. Tony was deeply superstitious, particularly about birds, but the place was too good to miss so we took it.

Things started to go wrong almost from the day we moved in. Perhaps having a proper house brought home to Tony the reality that it was time to settle down and face up to the muddle that we had so swiftly run away from. Perhaps the presence of the telephone made us accessible to the outside world, and the empty garage reminded us that we would need the car and driver. Perhaps the huge garden made us feel that we needed a gardener to keep it in trim. Or perhaps it was just the atmosphere of the house. I don't know, but nothing was quite the same as it had been in that shabby little flat. Tony began to drink more. It didn't help matters that the living room had a large built-in bar, with racks for wine and optics for bottles, a constant reminder of his problem. The honeymoon was over.

Tony phoned his agent, his mother, the chauffeur; I phoned John. We were both needed in London. I had to see how John was faring; Tony had to see his agent. There were offers of work, things to sign, to face up to.

The driver came to collect us. He had exchanged the car for a Mercedes, small, navy blue and classy. *That* was an improvement at any rate. We stayed in Tony's Knightsbridge flat – it was bare but very grand. No trace of Freddie was left – all her things had gone. Nevertheless I felt like an intruder.

I went to see John. He was gentle and kind as usual and

bearing up well. It was difficult to talk to him; there was so much I couldn't say and we had always been so truthful. My home seemed so cosy and comforting after the starkness of the Knightsbridge flat. The wardrobes were full of my clothes and my toilet things were still on the dressing table and in the bathroom, as if everything was waiting for me to return.

After a week in London we went home, Tony had purchased an expensive record player and packed all his records. He bought one for my parents at the same time. Very excited about it, he rang my father to tell him. 'Any records you would like me to buy for you, Fred?' he asked.

'That's very nice of you, Tony,' said Dad. 'Got a pen handy?'

'Right, I'm ready,' said Tony.

'"Green Door", by Frankie Vaughan, that's my first choice. Gene Autrey, the yodelling cowboy, singing "Tumbling Tumbleweed". Ann Ziegler and Webster Booth, "Wanting You" . . .'

The penny dropped. Tony threw the pad and pen over his shoulder. 'Got me at it, you bastard.'

We arrived at my parents' house, Tony slightly the worse for wear, happy to be out of London and keen to set up the expensive record player that he had so generously bought for them. That night I noticed something that had never occurred to me before. Tony was jealous of David. Whenever David and I were talking together, Tony would interrupt us and put himself between us, almost elbowing David aside. He vied for attention like a child himself. Of course, that's what happened when he was drunk: the child in him completely took over and dominated the other facets of his character, the serious, sensitive, shy side of him. To be honest, the childish part of him was the part I loved best. It matched the child in me that wanted to play and laugh and be irresponsible. That's why we had loved that silly flat: it was playing – not serious, like the house.

Anyway, we were stuck with the house, and that was that. We set up the record player and unpacked all the albums that Tony had brought from his London flat. He had a large collection of modern jazz, lots of Ella Fitzgerald, Sarah Vaughan, Carmen MacCrea – he liked women vocalists. He was a great romantic about music, and when he liked a song he would play it over and over again. We had a special favourite called 'Here's That Rainy Day', very sad and haunting. We came to believe that it was our bad-luck song but in spite of the fact that it was added to our list of superstitions we still played it more than any other.

We tried to settle into a routine. David would bring his friends to play after school and would stay at weekends, but I was reluctant to move him in permanently. Tony was drinking more and more, and the only part of the house that occupied his attention was the bar and seeing that it was well stocked. And his jealousy of David was becoming more and more apparent. My fears were well founded.

One evening I invited David and my parents to dinner. When we had finished eating, Tony, who had been drinking heavily throughout the meal, produced a bottle of brandy from under the bar. My heart froze. Cicely had warned me to try to keep him away from brandy. 'He turns into a killer on the stuff,' she said. How right she was!

After putting away two or three brandies in rapid succession, Tony turned on my mother. 'You Mancunian bitch!' he said, his face distorted and cold.

It wasn't a word to bring pleasure to my father's heart, but seeing the state that Tony was in, he didn't make an issue of it. All he said was, 'I think it's time to leave. Come on, Mother, get your coat.'

Deeply ashamed, I rang for a taxi, collected David from the garden, where mercifully he had been playing, and saw them off, while Tony sat on at the table glowering and knocking back the brandy.

After they had left I let him have it. 'How dare you talk to my mother like that,' I shouted at him, enraged by his rudeness. I snatched the bottle from the table, headed for the kitchen with it and started to pour it down the sink.

It was a bad move. With the speed of light he rushed after me, grabbed the bottle and, seeing that it was empty, flung it against the wall. 'You stupid bitch,' he snarled. 'That cost a lot of money.' The child in him had turned into a monster.

I was angry too, and frightened, but I stood up to him. 'You are never going to bring that stuff into the house again,' I said through clenched teeth. 'If you do, I shall leave you.'

His face turned purple with rage. 'You parochial cow,' he roared. 'Don't you give me orders.' And with that he rushed back into the living room, panting like a wounded bull, picked up a heavy iron coffee table, raised it above his head and went to fling it through the french windows. Quick as a flash I grabbled the table and pulled it backwards, and the three of us crashed to the floor. There was a shocked silence. Tony's hand was trapped under the table and badly cut, but the rage in us had passed and the pain in his hand had sobered him up.

'I do love these quiet after-dinner chats,' said Tony out of the silence.

For once I was too upset to laugh. I burst into tears.

After I recovered I cleaned him up and bandaged his hand. Then, contrite and apologetic, he helped me clear up the wreckage.

It was the first of many ugly scenes brought about by his escalating need for alcohol. In desperation I telephoned his mother Lily and asked her to visit us and try to talk some sense into him. The chauffeur brought her down to Broadstairs in the Mercedes. It was fortunate they were there, for that same night Tony went over the top completely. He drank himself into a coma which resulted in his having to be admitted into the nursing home in Highgate for a dry-out. So after a nightmare rush up the motorway with me in the back of the car holding a semicomatose Tony, I thankfully handed him over to the medical staff, after which Lily and I booked into a nearby hotel, where I sank into a deep and tearful sleep.

The next morning I had a meeting with Tony's psychiatrist, who outlined the treatment Tony needed. It consisted of deep sedation, vitamin therapy and electric shock therapy, all of which had been given before and none of which was a replacement for willpower. He told me that Freddie's suicide attempts had done Tony irreparable harm and stressed the need for him to feel secure in his relationship with me. He advised me to warn Tony that if he ever drank I would leave him, and if ever he did I must at all costs carry out my threat. I was allowed to see him and sit with him in his room during the next two days, while massive doses of Plurentavite, a strong mixture of vitamins, was injected into him to prevent liver damage. To this day the smell of vitamin B brings back the memory of that occasion and many more which were to follow.

Tony was very contrite and begged me not to tell him what happened. He promised never to drink again and vowed to make it up to me. We reiterated our vows to each other, and I swore that I would stay by him through thick and thin as long as he kept off alcohol.

After that he was put under heavy sedation for two days and I wasn't allowed to see him. I used the time to visit John and see that his affairs were in order at home. He was shocked by my appearance – I had lost a lot of weight since I had left him – and he took me out to dinner two nights running, to fatten me up he said gently. I told him that Tony was having vitamin treatment, but said nothing about what had happened. Always the gentleman, he asked me no awkward questions. How much part of me longed to go back to the comfort and serenity of my life with him and how much I valued him are difficult to describe in the light of what I was doing. But my love for Tony hadn't dimmed by one iota and that was what gave me the strength to go back and see it out.

After the deep sleep treatment came the electric shock therapy. I was allowed to be there when Tony came round. He was like a zombie; he didn't know who I was or where he was. He just lay there looking like a vegetable, staring at me with empty eyes. It was very sad to see him like that, so helpless and bovine. But gradually his health returned, helped by his massively strong constitution, and the day came when he was released into my care.

His doctor gave me bottles of pills – vitamins, Antabuse, sleeping pills and tranquillizers, with strict instructions to make sure he took one Antabuse every morning until such times as he could depend on his own willpower. If taken with alcohol these pills cause such a revulsion that even the smell of booze can bring on violent sickness and vomiting. Tony was not to eat cheese while he was taking them, as that could have the same effect.

While I was waiting for Tony in the foyer of the nursing home, a porter struck up a conversation with me. He started telling me about all the failures who had passed in and out of those portals. Apparently one patient, on the day of his release, had almost beaten his wife to death and then thrown himself off a railway bridge in front of a train.

'They always come back,' the porter said cheerfully.

Not this one, mate, I vowed silently to the tactful fellow.

We moved back to the Knightsbridge flat. It seemed wiser to stay in London for a while, to be near medical help in case anything went wrong. After what had taken place in Broadstairs I had gone off the Coq d'Or, thinking maybe it *was* a bad-luck house after all. Besides, there were more distractions in London to take Tony's mind off the need to drink. So, after staying in bed for two days watching television and making love a great deal, we planned a list of outings – art galleries, theatres and cinemas. Tony had the most irritating habit of changing his mind at the last minute. No sooner was I dressed and ready to go than he would want to stay in and watch something on TV, or he would want to make love just as I had got my make-up on. His intensity and demands for sex frightened us both slightly and we tried to cut down a bit. 'I'm going to draw an imaginary line down the middle of this bed, over which no tits, arses or willies must stray,' he said. But it didn't work, and I was no help at all – I found him irresistible.

We were having dinner one night in a little restaurant at the far end of Kensington High Street. I had been shopping that afternoon and had bought a garter. They had come fleetingly back into fashion along with the mini skirt. The thought of it turned Tony on like mad, so spotting a pretty white lace one in Harrods, I bought it, put it in my hand-bag and forgot about it. I came across it in the cloakroom of the restaurant and slipped it on. We had finished our first course and were looking into each other's eyes while waiting for the main course to arrive.

'I bought you a present when I was out shopping today,' I said, and gave him a quick flash of the garter.

'Stone me,' said Tony, 'you might have waited until I'd eaten my chicken.' He signalled the waiter, asked for the bill, and in seconds I was rushed out of the restaurant under the startled gaze of the manager, who asked anxiously if there was anything wrong with the food. 'I just remembered we've left something in the oven,' said Tony, and I was bundled into a taxi and rushed off home.

'The next time you pull something like that on me, do it *after* dinner,' he said. 'I was looking forward to my chicken *suprême*.'

There were days, however, when he sank so deeply into depression that I could almost see a blue cloud around him. Nothing I could say would penetrate it. That was when his longing to escape behind a comforting curtain of alcohol surpassed his love for me, the distraction of sex or any form of entertainment known to man. It was something that he couldn't talk to me about. I wasn't an alcoholic. I could take a drink or leave it alone, and seeing what it had done to him, I preferred to leave it alone. The only people who could understand that intense need were other alcoholics. So there were days when we were estranged from each other by his craving, and he would sit looking out of the window, his back hunched, like a small boy forbidden to go out to play.

I was wise enough not to attempt to jolly him out of those moods or to sympathize with him. The last thing he ever wanted was sympathy – he was far too proud for that. But I never left him alone in the flat during those times; that would have been downright dangerous. So I would potter about in the kitchen or try to bury myself in a book until the mood changed. Then he'd say, 'Come on, let's go to the pictures,' or 'Let's go for a walk.' (Going out for a walk with him was always a worry as he was so easily recognized).

One afternoon we went to see *The Wrong Box*, in which Peter Sellers played the part of a shady North Country alcoholic doctor. In one scene he said, 'I wasn't always as you see me now. In the old days the sick and the groggy would come to me from miles around.' This rendered Tony helpless with laughter throughout the rest of the film. 'The sick and the groggy,' he kept saying, mopping his eyes. 'Oh dear, the sick and the groggy.' It became one of his favourite expressions, but he didn't laugh at the end of the film in the scene in which he himself appeared. He didn't even mention it. He was always so generous in his praise of other performers and so hard on himself.

The day came when he announced that he wanted to move away from London and go back to the bungalow. My heart sank. I dreaded going back there but he was adamant. 'There's no use having a bloody house and not living in it,' he argued. Although I dreaded the place, I wanted to see David, so we moved back.

By the second day the novelty had already worn off. Tony was restless and edgy and refused to take his Antabuse tablet. I panicked and pleaded with him. With the cunning of the alcoholic, Tony insisted that the crisis had passed. He didn't need them any more. They were bad for him if he took them for long periods of time and they made him feel nauseous. There was nothing else I could do without making a scene and that had to be avoided at all costs.

'Why don't you make a nice *fillet de boeuf en croûte*?'

Tony suggested. 'We'll have a cosy dinner by candlelight to celebrate being home.'

We were being served in the butcher's when Tony, with impeccable timing, said, 'Wait for me here, I'm bursting for a pee,' and fled. Shaking with nerves, I waited outside the butcher's shop for fifteen minutes. Tony returned with a carrier bag from a local wine merchants. He was wearing a broad grin. He kissed me soundly and held the bag out to me, as if he were giving me the most wonderful gift in the world.

'This is for you to drink with dinner.'

'I don't want it,' I said through gritted teeth.

He looked like a child who had been rejected.

'Don't want it?' He was deeply hurt. 'It's a Château Margaux '57 – cost me the earth.'

So, biting back the obvious retort, I accepted the unwanted gift with grave foreboding.

On the way home I noticed that his breath smelled strongly of peppermint.

He was ingratiatingly loving throughout the rest of the day, but restless. As I was preparing the dinner that evening he grabbed his coat and made for the door. 'I'm just popping out for a bit – to join the library,' he said, and was off like a bat out of hell.

'At seven-thirty at night?' I asked an empty room.

I went on cooking, salting the pastry with the tears that ran unchecked down my face, not knowing what else to do in his absence, remembering the promise I had made to the doctor to leave him if he had another drink and not wanting to keep it. He was back in an hour, his face flushed, another carrier bag in his hand.

'More presents?' I inquired bitterly.

When he saw my red-rimmed eyes his own filled with tears. 'Please try to understand,' he begged me. 'I needed a drink tonight. It's only wine. I can control it, I promise.'

So I mopped my eyes, lit the candles, accepted a glass of wine and served the dinner. In between the dry-outs and the time when his drinking reached a dangerously high peak, when he still had it under control, he was wonderful company, and that night he was at his best, recharging my glass, which I emptied rapidly, reasoning that the more I drank, the less there would be for him.

Looking back, I seem to have suffered more anxiety and tension when he was dry than when he was drinking, because then not only did I have to endure his terrible depressions, but I also lived in dread of the day when I smelled that first tell-tale hint of alcohol on his breath and listened to his lies. At least when it was out in the open the problem was more tangible.

So on that particular night I temporarily laid aside the problem, drowned the dread of the future in a fine old wine, and gave myself up to the pleasure of being entertained by one of the greatest and most loved personalities that England will ever know. There I sat in the candlelight, a one-woman, deeply loved audience, as Tony held me spellbound with impersonations of Sid Field, told me wonderful anecdotes from his past, and changed the tears of sorrow that I had shed earlier into tears of laughter.

Once again things went smoothly for a while. Tony drank wine at dinner in the evenings and a few beers at lunchtime. He was in control, his old boyish self again. Then Dorothy Squires, who would visit my parents from time to time, rang us one day to say that she was doing a week at Swansea. She suggested that Tony and I should take David down there to see the show and stay over on the Saturday night. David adored Dorothy. He had already spent a week's holiday with her during the summer while she was doing cabaret in her native Wales, and during each performance she would bring David on stage with her to sing a song. This had brought the house down. David had a sweet voice and looked like an angel. He was mad with excitement at the prospect of seeing her again.

We set off in the Mercedes very early on the Saturday morning, planning to miss the motorways if possible and have a leisurely lunch *en route*. David had bought Dorothy a gift and was brimming over with pleasure and anticipation. I, of course, should have realized that I had two small boys in the car, and one of them was being left out.

At our first stop a few miles out of Ramsgate we had breakfast, Tony's accompanied by a glass of champagne perry.

'It's a bit early for that isn't it?' I asked.

'It's like drinking lemonade,' Tony assured me, and ordered another. Two more were consumed at another road house half an hour later.

'We'll never get there by tonight at this rate,' I said anxiously.

By the time we stopped for lunch we had made five stops, and I realized to my horror that the drinks were being reinforced by brandy. By the time we sat down to lunch Tony was drunk and unpleasant with it. He kept glaring at David and people were beginning to stare at us.

The first course arrived. Tony had orderd *escargots*.

'Yuk,' said David.

Tony's face darkened even more. 'What do you mean, "Yuk?" You ungrateful little bastard,' he said loudly. 'These are delicious. Go on, eat one.' With that he grabbed David by the chin and tried to force a snail into his mouth.

That was enough for me. 'Leave him alone,' I said.

David was by now in tears and wiping the grease off his mouth. Tony grabbed him by the chin again. 'There's not a tear in the little bastard's eyes. Look at him, Mother's little darling.'

I jumped up, pushed him away from David and turned to the driver. 'Take us to the nearest station, please, right now. And then you can come back and take this *thing* wherever he wants to go. We're going home.'

By now David was sobbing with fear and disappointment. I put my arms around him and hurried him out of the restaurant, my brain racing. I wanted to put as much space as I could between Tony and us. The only problem was that I hadn't any money for the train fare.

Tony came lurching after us. He tried to pull David away from me.

'Leave him alone,' I sobbed. 'You're a monster.'

Tony realized that, once more, he had gone too far, but it was too late to make amends. It was one thing to attack me, but another to bully my son, who hadn't deserved any of it.

The driver, who had hurriedly settled the bill, joined us outside the restaurant.

'Take us to the nearest station,' I shouted at him, in a complete panic to get David and myself away from this dreadful situation.

The man opened the car door and I pulled David into the back seat, cradling him in my arms, while Tony fell into the front alongside the driver.

'Take us home,' Tony said in a thick voice. And home we came from our pleasant little outing, with David and me clinging to each other and sobbing quietly in the back of the car. Tony attempted to stroke David from time to time but I, fearful of Tony's unstable condition, pushed his hand away and held my son even closer.

When we eventually drew up outside my parents' house I leaned over the front seat, held up my finger in front of Tony's face and said menacingly, 'Don't you *dare* try to follow me into the house,' and Tony, knowing I was deadly serious, didn't.

'What has that dreadful man done to you?' asked Mother, seeing our white and tear-stained faces. But Dad, being more compassionate, simply put his arms around me while I sobbed into his shoulder.

David, in spite of the disappointment of having his weekend ruined, ended up comforting me. 'I know he loves you, Mum,' he said with infinite understanding, and I knew it too.

Later that evening the phone rang. It was Tony, mumbling drunkenly that he wanted me to come home. I refused and hung up. Later still the driver came to tell me that Stanley Gibbon, an old friend of Tony's, had been sent for to look after him as Tony was in a bad way. Unable to turn my back on him, despite my mother's protestations, I went back to the bungalow.

Tony was sleeping deeply – he was almost in a coma. He had knocked back a lot more booze. We decided to take him back to the nursing home. I rang the psychiatrist on his emergency number and told him what had happened. He was very angry. 'You should have left him as soon as he took that first drink,' he told me. 'He has got to believe that you mean what you say. Send him up immediately and stay out of sight. You've got to make him think that he has lost you.'

It didn't seem right to desert Tony when he was in that condition, but I did as I was told. I packed his things and Stanley and the driver took him to London. I had arranged with the psychiatrist that I should move back to the Knightsbridge flat to be on hand if and when Tony needed me. It was a ghastly business, hiding in another room while the two men half carried Tony out to the car, and then being left in that silent house to tidy up the wreckage of the day. I did the best I could, but the place frightened me, so I hurriedly left a note for the cleaner, saying that we had been called away unexpectedly, rang for a taxi and fled back to the comfort and safety of Ramsgate.

I had a hard time explaining to my despairing parents why I was still determined to stick it out. Eventually I crept into bed to be cuddled and comforted by my nine-year-old son, who, in spite of all the terrible things that had happened, remained steadfastly devoted to Tony.

I stayed in Ramsgate on the Sunday. I felt reluctant to leave, wanting to make it up to David in some way. The next morning he brought me up a cup of tea, with instructions from my mother to have a good lie-in. 'She said it's a wonder that her hair hasn't turned white overnight,' he giggled, and I thanked God that he at least didn't seem to bear any resentment against me or Tony.

When I arrived at the Knightsbridge flat on the Wednesday morning I immediately rang the nursing home in

Highgate, to be told by the psychiatrist that Tony was being uncooperative, refusing to be sedated, and demanding to know my whereabouts. He'd had to be physically restrained from using the telephone on more than one occasion. There was a slightly hysterical edge to the doctor's voice. However, he still insisted that I should stay out of sight, although I argued against it. It made no sense to me to stay away when it was obviously causing Tony such distress, let alone the staff at the nursing home. But the doctor was adamant, insisting that if I didn't stick to my guns Tony would walk all over me in future and that my word would mean nothing to him.

I gave way, reasoning that the doctor had been through all this many times before with Tony and Freddie. But at the back of my mind I realized that he had not managed to effect a lasting cure, in spite of all his experience. I knew Tony well enough by now to recognize his iron will and his bull-like stubbornness. If he had made up his mind it would take more than a few injections to change it.

I was given strict instructions not to answer the telephone unless there was a coded ring, which we agreed in advance, and to warn my parents to say that they had no idea where I was should Tony manage to gain access to a telephone and call them. This seemed a shoddy subterfuge to me, but I did as I was told.

Two mornings later I was awakened from a deep sleep by the telephone ringing at the side of the bed. Taken off guard, I answered it. The phone went dead. Thinking that it was probably a wrong number, I went back to sleep. The next time I opened my eyes Tony was standing by the bed looking down at me with an angry, hurt expression on his face. Still befuddled by sleep, my first reaction was to give a welcoming smile. That was all that was needed to change the hurt look on his expressive face to one of relief and joy, followed swiftly by boyish reproach.

'Why did you hide from me?' he asked.

'Don't you *know*, Tony?' I answered, exasperated. 'Have you really forgotten?'

And of course he had – he remembered little of what took place during his bouts of heavy drinking and hated to be told. But this time I let him have it, in detail, while he sat on the bed wincing with shame.

'Poor little David,' he said. 'Poor little bugger. I'll make it up to him,' he promised, 'only don't leave me. I can't face going through that treatment without you there.'

So, all too ready to believe that things would work out this time, I moved over in the bed while he joyfully divested himself of his clothes with the speed of a quick-change artist, and under the covers, surrounded by the all too familiar smell of vitamin B, we planned his next attempt at a comeback into the world of sobriety.

Ten

Tony completed his treatment at home, visiting the psychiatrist in Highgate for therapy and to finish his course of vitamin injections. We gave up the Broadstairs house. I had never liked it. Tony blamed it on the cock motifs, as usual using superstition as an excuse when things went wrong. Whenever he came off a drinking bout he tried to relieve his guilt and atone for his overindulgences by embarking on a Scrooge-like economy drive. As the lease on the Knightsbridge flat was due for renewal, he decided to make a clean sweep and give that up as well, to my great relief. So we went flat hunting to find something new, without memories – an unfurnished place which we could furnish together, where we could wipe the slate clean, and begin our new life.

As the Knightsbridge flat was vastly overpriced, our search was limited by the need for economy. We concentrated on looking for something in a less fashionable area, and found one less than a ten-minute walk away from Barons Court. As I was still in close contact with John, this was all to the good. It had the added advantage of being almost opposite our favourite restaurant.

When we went into the foyer on our first visit, however, Tony clutched my arm and said in a voice of doom. 'Oh dear, this won't do.'

'Why ever not?' I asked.

'Bird pictures,' he said, pointing to the walls. 'All over the bloody place.'

'Tony,' I said, 'this is the entrance hall. We won't have

them in our flat.' I managed to persuade him to look at the flat at least.

It turned out to be just right for us. It had two bed-rooms, one of which Tony could use as a study. He was thinking of writing a rather spiritual book, which was going to be called *The Link*.

The flat also had two lavatories, which was handy, as Tony was very embarrassed about lavatory noises. When-ever he needed to go, he would pick up the transistor radio with a glazed look in his eyes, while I would disappear to the other end of the flat. It was his only modesty. If he farted he would say, 'Are you sure you really want to carry on with this?' I would answer, 'Yes, farts and all.'

As the lease on the Knightsbridge flat was due to expire before Christmas and the new flat, which needed painting, wouldn't be ready until January, Tony booked a service flat in Dolphin Square for a few weeks to bridge the gap. We went to have a look at the place before we moved in. The flat itself was ugly, and to Tony's dismay, it had a green and cream tiled kitchen and bathroom. Green was worse than birds.

'It's God's colour,' I argued. 'Are trees unlucky? Is grass?'

'It's not a superstition about green. It's a fact. I bought Cis an emerald ring and everything went wrong from then on,' he insisted, unable to accept the fact that it would have made no difference.

However, to compensate for the green, Dolphin Square had lots of advantages. There was a small shopping arcade, an efficient reception area with helpful porters, a sports complex with a large swimming pool, a restaurant and, not so reassuring from my point of view, a well-stocked bar. But after the last débâcle Tony had promised, 'If continuing to drink means losing you there is no contest.' So I stilled the little pangs of anxiety. To celebrate finding the flat we had a drink in the bar. I let him buy me a bloody mary and he had a tomato juice with lots of Worcester sauce. 'Honestly,' he said, smacking his lips over his drink,

'I get just as much pleasure out of a tomato juice.'

Christmas was approaching. Strange as it may seem, I was going to Ramsgate with John to have a normal family Christmas. Tony had arranged to stay with Lily in Bournemouth.

The week before Christmas we went for lunch in a little Italian restaurant just up the road from the Knightsbridge flat. We had been there many times before and were on first-name terms with the waiters. On this particular day the restaurant was decorated with a Christmas tree bedecked with pound notes and the odd fiver. The money was being collected to buy a film projector for the children's ward of a local hospital.

Tony went to the bar to get his customary tomato juice.

'Sauce as usual?' inquired the waiter.

'Yes, lots of sauce,' said my friend, and he carried the drink over to our table. 'You know, I've just remembered something,' he said. He was in a particular good mood that morning. 'I've got a movie camera and a screen at home. I only used the camera once, on a trip up the Rhine, and when the film was developed I found that I'd filmed the whole thing with the lens cover on, so I lost interest. I'll give it to the hospital.' He downed his tomato juice in one gulp. 'In fact, I'll go and get it right now, I won't be a minute. Wait here and look at the menu.' He left me at the table.

It was while I was waiting that I realized the dregs in the bottom of his glass were too watery. I sniffed it. Sauce, eh? My heart plummeted. He was at it again.

When he returned I watched him hand over the generous gift with a flourish.

'Have a drink on me,' said the grateful patron. 'The usual? With sauce?' And then there was some clever sleight of hand under the bar. I seethed inwardly.

He returned to the table with his bloody mary.

'I'm so proud of you,' I said smiling warmly.

'The way you've kicked the booze and taken to tomato juice has really impressed me.'

He grinned modestly. 'Yes, I think I've kicked it this time,' he said, taking a swig of his drink. 'I don't think you'll ever see me take another drink.'

'You mean, after you've finished that bloody mary, you lying, cheating bastard,' I hissed.

The smile was wiped from his face, to be replaced by the lost-dog expression that I found hard to resist. 'Have I behaved badly?' he argued. 'I can handle the odd bloody mary. It's mostly tomato juice anyway. Don't leave me because of one small lapse. It's been good lately, hasn't it?'

It had been good, I had to admit. 'But it will accelerate just like before,' I said.

'Not this time, I'm not putting you through all that again.' He went on pleading and promising until again I said I would stay.

The next day the owner of the restaurant called to tell us that the hospital, the beneficiary of his generous gift, had asked if he would visit the children's ward personally. He not only agreed but offered to give each child a present. Armed with a list of the children's names and ages, Marion and I set off for the shops. Back at the flat we wrapped each gift in different coloured paper according to age and sex of the recipient. A few days later the three of us went to the hospital.

On arrival we were taken to the matron's office. At the sight of the loaded drinks trolley, my heart sank.

'Would you like a drink, Mr Hancock?' asked the matron.

'A Scotch, please,' said Mr Hancock, rubbing his hands together and avoiding my eye.

Marion and I exchanged worried looks.

We went to see the children and distributed the gifts, after which the matron told us that she had arranged a special lunch party as a thank-you for all that Tony had done. The lunch was a gala occasion, attended by members of the hospital staff.

We were served apéritifs and over lunch Tony was amusing, expansive and thirsty. He refused to meet my eye. There was nothing I could do without causing embarrassment; I had to go along with the whole thing, making small talk and laughing indulgently, while across the room Tony guzzled down booze. I wanted to charge at him and slap the smug, self-satisfied look off his face.

'My old people would love to meet you, Mr Hancock,' said the matron over coffee. 'They need companionship much more than the children do.'

'Delighted,' said Tony, beaming with goodwill and alcohol. 'Lead on, madam,' he said, draining his brandy. Off we trailed, Marion and I, by now full of dread, behind the matron and an increasingly arrogant Tony.

The visit was a nightmare as Tony strutted about the wards. We covered the whole hospital, meeting people who were dying of cancer and others who were lonely and old. Some of whom had been rejected by their families. One old lady of ninety clutched a box of Maltesers; they had been sent by her son who couldn't be bothered to visit her for Christmas. Another, struggling to eat her dinner with arthritic hands, beamed with joy at meeting the great Hancock. 'I'll feed you,' said the good-natured buffoon, and he nearly choked her in his clumsiness.

What an ordeal it was. These people, who were ill and lonely, were being patronized by this man who had the world at his feet, who was loved by thousands, and who was behaving with total insensitivity to the plight of those around him. Mercifully the visit lurched to its close. It had turned into a party for Tony, the reasons for going completely forgotten. Meanwhile Marion and I had grown more and more depressed by the sadness and hardship we had seen and more and more angry at the way Tony was behaving.

In the car on the way home he rounded on me, his eyes cold and unfriendly. 'You were a bloody misery,' he said. 'I had to do all the bloody work.'

I gasped at the unfairness of his remark and something exploded inside me. I called him an unfeeling, drunken bastard and told him about the people he had seen and not noticed. Then I told him what I had given up for him, while he mocked me, calling me a gutless prig with no staying power. We were both out of control, incensed with anger. Poor Marion sat with her head bowed wishing she could escape. Tony told the driver to stop at the nearest pub. As he got out of the car he shouted, 'Go back to your nice safe home then, you self-righteous bitch. I've had a lucky escape.' He slammed the car door and disappeared into the pub.

I stayed with Marion that night, sick with disappointment that the day which had started out so well because of Tony's generosity and good intent, should have gone so disastrously wrong, and wondering where he was and how he was feeling.

So our first Christmas was to be spent apart, in mutual rejection. It seemed impossible to believe that in the past four months my contented, happy life had been turned upside down. I had been shaken to my roots.

The next day I went to Ramsgate with John. I said nothing about what had happened. I was still angry with Tony and full of remorse about what I had done to John, wishing that I could erase the last four months from my memory. But I couldn't. I was simply getting tougher. My anger was my self-defence. It inured me to Tony at times, giving me a momentary respite before I girded my loins and rushed back into the fray, leaving my loved ones standing helplessly by, all of them hurt and bewildered by my hopeless devotion to Tony.

Christmas passed pleasantly. The family were glad to get me back and I was glad to be there, resting and comfortable, taking long walks with John and David, talking about everything except the one thing uppermost in our minds.

The only person who understood how I felt was David. In spite of all that Tony had done to him, he was still firmly on Tony's side. With a child's clarity he saw through all the grown-up logic and sensed that what was between us was real. If I hadn't had his support I don't think I could have gone on with it, but, like me, he recognized and loved the real person who was struggling to emerge from the alcohol-damaged part of himself.

I told John of my intention to stick it out, and after Christmas we left for London together. John had to go on location immediately and I went to stay with Marion. As soon as I arrived she told me that the doctor who looked after the artists attached to the Delfont Agency had left a phone number. I was to ring him as soon as possible.

The doctor told me that Tony was in a bad way and desperate for me to help him. He was prepared to have another dry-out. He had made the usual promises. With the help of a specialist, the doctor proposed to treat him in the flat at Dolphin Square. I told the doctor that I would do anything, as long as Tony tried to help himself, but that I could no longer put up with the deceit. I asked him to pass that message on.

Apparently Tony had taken up with a couple who lived at Dolphin Square. The man and his wife, both hard drinkers, had been delighted to help Tony drink himself blind. The three of them had had a high old time of it before Tony had once more gone over the top.

I had no idea exactly what had happened in Dolphin Square over the Christmas period; I didn't want to know. Nor did I know what was to be demanded of me. I was to become Tony's nurse, gaoler and bodyguard. He had elected to stay in the small flat because of the conveniences. The fact that there were porters, shops and room service made him feel less isolated. As it turned out, they were a mixed blessing.

I moved in, Tony looked a little more crumpled than when I had last seen him. Again he was contrite and loving, but I was stronger now, more on my guard and less forgiving. The doctor and the specialist arranged to give him deep sleep and vitamin therapy. They explained that he would spend most of the time under sedation – all I would be required to do was to keep him company and feed him between rests.

They prescribed Largactil and barbiturates, but the combination went disastrously wrong, with the result that he didn't sleep at all. His resistance to sleeping pills was massive. If I had taken one sixth of his nightly dose of barbiturates I would have been in a coma for a week but, like most alcoholics, Tony was an insomniac – it needed an almost fatal dose to knock him out.

The mixture of drugs affected his brain and made him completely dotty. Fortunately in his dementia he became childlike and benign. Wherever he had retired to in his mind, he was having a whale of a time. But for me it was like having a large sleepless child on my hands, who couldn't be left alone for a moment.

I found in the awful days that followed that his humour was an inherent part of his make-up; in the midst of his lunacy he could still be hilariously funny. Sometimes he thought we were on a plane. He would look out of the window and say, 'Look, the plane's hovering over Manchester. See how still we are.' Then 'Fuck it, what do we want to go to Manchester for?' and he'd grab the phone and say to the bewildered switchboard operator, 'Front cabin here. Take us on to Paris.'

The doctor warned the switchboard to ignore the odd calls emanating from our flat. But he was becoming increasingly worried by Tony's behaviour. He said the dottiness would wear off, but it was taking a hell of a time.

Meanwhile Tony remained in transit. 'Front cabin here. Bring us a bottle of Dom Perignon' was the most frequent request. I would go to the kitchen and make him a drink of tonic water with a dash of ginger in it, and bring it in on a tray. 'You can't beat this Dom Perignon,' he'd say, smacking his lips. It was like humouring a large, playful St Bernard dog.

Sometimes he thought we were in Paris; he would want to go sightseeing and try to leave the flat. I would restrain him gently, humouring him, afraid he might turn violent. 'We can't leave yet,' I'd say, 'Lily's on her way round' or 'There's something good on TV. Let's watch it first and then go out.'

Marion and Dinny came over. I was becoming dotty myself by this time and hallucinating from lack of sleep. Dinny could physically prevent Tony from escaping while I grabbed a half an hour's rest in the bedroom.

Three days passed and three sleepless nights, and apart from the odd catnap, when I would gratefully sink down beside him and pass into oblivion, Tony was still on his feet.

The crunch came on the fourth night. He actually said that he wanted to go to sleep. He undressed and got into bed. Dizzy with relief, I joined him. The next thing I knew I opened my eyes from a dreamless sleep to find him standing at the foot of the bed supported by two porters. He was giggling like a naughty schoolboy, stark naked except for a jockstrap, which was on back to front, and a green candlewick bedspread. He had escaped while I slept and had suddenly appeared in the restaurant downstairs. To make matters worse, it was New Year's Eve and the place was crowded with revellers. At this odd apparition a woman had screamed. He had gone over to her and pointing to his willy, had said, 'I don't suppose you've ever seen one of these before, madam.' Then the porters had grabbed him and ushered him out.

Tony's version was that he had been shopping and bought a shawl for Lily. Then he'd put in on and gone to have a drink. 'I heard a woman scream, and when I looked down, someone had cut the end of my jockstrap,' he said indignantly. 'Luckily the boys here got me out before there was a nasty scene.'

It was the last straw. The next morning I asked to see the specialist and demanded he should arrange for a night nurse to help look after Tony. I had to have some rest. I was dreaming standing up, exhausted from continually leading Tony away from the phone and away from the front door. The specialist, whose name was Mr Merryman and who only handled alcoholics gave me some news that was anything but merry. He said that he could only take on twelve patients, because they were a full-time responsibility, and that Tony was farther gone than any of them. 'There's no more than a one per cent chance of saving him,' he said. 'My advice to you is to save yourself.' Why no one suggested Alcoholics Anonymous I do not know. It was the only thing that might have worked, I realize now. But knowing Tony and his paranoid need for privacy, I doubt whether he would have been able to reveal his inner self to others. His fame isolated him from the help that would have been available to him. So there was nothing left but hope.

The night nurse arrived. My heart sank at the sight of him. He was short and thin. I'd wanted a navvy. But he was efficient, firm and calm, and I got my first night's sleep.

The next morning, by some miracle, Tony had got his brains back in place. The relief at having him back was so great it reduced me to tears. The doctor arrived; he was also vastly relieved to find Tony back to normal. He said the worst was over. After he left, Tony felt hungry. He fancied scrambled eggs, and leaving him sitting up in bed, I went to the kitchen. While I was preparing the food I heard a strange choking sound from the bedroom. I dropped what I was doing and rushed through. Tony was foaming at the mouth, his face blue and distorted. He was having a convulsive fit. Thinking it was a heart attack, I began to shake. I managed to ring downstairs. 'Send someone up quickly and get the doctor,' I shouted. The porters were there in no time, helping me to hold his thrashing body until the convulsions subsided. As he came round, his eyes focused on me and he tried to reach out, but he had no strength. He couldn't speak for a while. He looked ghastly. I clung to his hand, shaking uncontrollably, trying unsuccessfully to hold back the sobs.

His first words were, 'You poor little sod.'

'I thought you were dying,' I said between sobs, while the porters gently cleaned him up and made some tea.

When the doctor returned he told me that Tony had had a liver attack. He gave him a Plurentavite injection.

Mr Merryman came later that day and gave Tony a stern talking to. 'If you don't stop drinking,' he said, 'you will be dead in less than three months.' Considerably shaken by what had happened, Tony agreed to do as he was told. We arranged to see the specialist every week to chart Tony's progress.

Mr Merryman was as concerned about my health as he was about Tony's. I had lost a stone since I met Tony and Mr Merryman put me on a course of vitamin injections to build me up. He warned me that I would have a hard time looking after Tony. Quite often, he said, those closest to an alcoholic succumb to drink themselves in order to cope with the strain. I assured him that, after what I'd seen in the past few months, there was no danger of that. Paradoxically, he said that if we went out to dinner a dry table made the problem more obvious. 'He has to learn to live in a world full of temptations, so it's best to treat alcohol casually. Let him order wine for you. He will feel less need that way.' He told me never to lecture Tony about what had happened, and to stay calm and constant when he was irritable or depressed. He ended by wishing me luck. 'You are going to need it,' he said ominously.

So, weak and shaky though we both were, we had come through another crisis. Tony's feeling for me seemed to have grown stronger: he was more affectionate and considerate, and I was more in love than ever. We moved into the new flat and set about making it into a home. At long last it seemed as if everything was going to be all right. We set about shopping with a vengeance, choosing furniture together. We had brought a few things with us from the Knightsbridge flat, but everything else was brand new, like my hopes for the future. Tony liked my taste and, apart from the study, which was to be his own private domain, I was given free rein.

We found a wonderful cleaner called Mary, who came every day. Tony hated to see me doing housework, except for cooking, which, as he was now completely dry, replaced his interest in alcohol. Under his supervision I would prepare complicated gourmet dinners, while he sat on a stool reading the instructions aloud.

He drank tea incessantly. Practically every half hour he would ask for tea. It replaced the need for something to drink. It was a ritual to fill in the gaps that booze had left in his life. Every morning Mary's first task was to bring us a tray of tea and toast, along with the morning papers – he ordered them all – and we would sit in bed reading out snatches of news to each other. 'Peanuts' was his favourite comic strip and Snoopy his most loved character. 'What's he done now?' he would ask.

'Well, his book's been sent back and he's suffering from rejection-slip shock,' I said once, showing him the picture of Snoopy lying in a coma on top of his kennel, his ears drooping dejectedly.

Tony chuckled his way through the day about that one. 'Rejection-slip shock,' he'd say suddenly. 'Oh dear, oh dear.' It became one of his favourite expressions. If he had the blues, he'd say he was suffering from rejection-slip shock. And, of course, he got the blues himself – someone who could laugh at life as wholeheartedly as Tony naturally saw its other side. He was an emotional pendulum, swinging from one extreme to the other. John described it like living on top of a shout.

When Tony was depressed he would go to his study and sit at his desk. His great work hadn't got under way. I would find him sitting dejectedly staring out of the window, the first page, headed 'The Link, or Anyone for Tennis? by Tony Hancock', waiting like a reproach in the typewriter. On the shelves his awards for Personality of the Year stared down at him with their empty eye sockets. 'Give us a clamp (his word for a hug), for God's sake,' the great man would say.

Sometimes, to cheer him up, I would try to get him to answer his fan mail. It still came in loads from all over the world. 'Just look at how loved you are,' I would say. But he was reluctant to open the letters. They reminded him too much of the past.

We sometimes ate out but usually we stayed at home, eating our dinner in bed in front of the television. Watching TV with Tony was a novel experience. He was the most wonderful audience. *Come Dancing* – his favourite programme – rendered him helpless with laughter. He'd hang over the side of the bed, gasping for breath, hurling pillows about in all directions. The bedroom was like a battlefield. As I attempted to remake the bed around him, he would flail about helplessly as something else caught his attention.

Occasionally he would go to Delfont's to see his agent and discuss the future. He still had many offers. There was talk about the possibility of him starring in a musical about Noah's Ark, by Leslie Bricusse. But, although he talked about it because he needed to feel he had a future, he was reluctant to undertake anything that would upset the quiet routine of our lives. As far as I was concerned, I would have been happy if he'd never worked again. Screw the world and his talent. For long periods I would forget that he was famous, until, in a theatre or restaurant I would suddenly realize that people were staring at us, and with a shock I would remember that he was a household name. Then I would become as shy as he was, deeply resentful at the instrusion on our privacy.

Sometimes David would come and stay for weekends and half-terms. We would take him to the zoo. Tony was potty about Guy the gorilla. On one occasion the keeper let us into the private section to feed him. I had some nuts and Guy held out his hand for them. He consumed them greedily, but when I offered him some ordinary animal food, he threw it away in disgust and turned his back on us. It touched Tony to see him moodily sitting there, being stared at by the crowds. 'Poor sod, I know what he feels like,' he said.

Tony also loved the penguins. According to him, they were always holding union meetings, due to their habit of standing around in groups. 'There's a heckler,' he'd say, pointing to a particularly noisy one. He gave them all human characteristics.

The attention he attracted always made these outings difficult – he would usually end up feeling like one of the inmates. Ironically, one of his favourite pastimes was watching people, but with a face as well known as his it was hard for him to go unnoticed. He would talk about wearing a disguise, a small moustache and dark glasses.

Once or twice we went to Ramsgate. We stayed in a hotel – things were a bit strained at home. My parents had told me that they lived in hope that I would go back to John, and although they accepted us, they found the shy, sober Tony almost harder to cope with than the affectionate, bear-hugging one.

So the months slipped by. They were the happiest times that I'd had with him and they gave me a taste of how things might have been. One night we had dinner at a restaurant just around the corner from Harley Street. It was small and intimate and many of the dishes were cooked at the table. On this occasion a guitarist had been hired to entertain the customers, not a very wise move in such a small room. Over dinner we were fascinated by his attempts to serenade people at their tables while trying to make himself as inconspicuous as possible and keep out of the way of the bustling waiters. Tony was spellbound, half hoping that there would be a collision. On the way home he began to form the idea for a sketch, with himself as a gypsy violinist, wearing a bandanna and cummerbund, getting into a muddle, his bow catching fire while a waiter attempted to cook a *crêpe suzette*, a customer lighting a cigarette from his flaming bow. By the faraway look in his eyes I knew that he was wanting to get out there again into the dangerous arena of show business.

He began negotiations with Delfont's to make a series for ABC TV. In April he started script conferences with John Muir and Eric Green. All began well. Tony stayed sober and worked to a strict timetable. For the first few weeks I could have set my clock by him. As soon as rehearsals were over he would ring to tell me that he was on his way home, and I would be by the phone waiting for his call. One evening the phone didn't ring at 5.30; by 6.30 my stomach was beginning to churn. The ominous feeling of dread that I had pushed to the back of my mind returned in full force. I knew he was drinking. There was nothing to do but wait. I was trying to watch TV when I heard the front door open quietly. I put out my hundredth cigarette. It was 8.30 – I'd looked at the clock enough times in the past three hours to know.

Tony was standing in the doorway of the living room with one arm behind his back, his eyes swimming with tears and a nauseating lovesick look on his face. 'I've let you down,' he said, and with a flourish he produced a large bunch of yellow roses from behind his back. He knelt down in front of me and put his head in my lap.

I felt his tears on my knee. I was crying now. I stroked his head. 'We'll start again tomorrow, it's all right. Don't be upset,' I said soothingly.

There was a long pause.

'I'm a bloody genius though,' he said with a chuckle from the depths of my lap. He looked up – his eyes bright. 'I really got them today.' He began to pace the room, describing what he'd done, full of himself and his achievements. Smug and swaggering, he swung round to face me, and I let him have it with the roses, beating him over the head until they disintegrated.

'You've got me at it, you bastard. You softened me up with these,' I roared. 'Do you know what I've been through? Do you know what you've done? You bloody piss artist.'

He stood there wincing as I belaboured him until my anger was spent. Then he rolled his eyes heavenwards. 'Stone me,' he said. 'I'm glad I didn't try to win you over with a bottle of champagne.'

Of course I laughed – it was impossible not to laugh at Tony. He was the funniest man I've ever known. No one else has ever made me laugh as much, or cry. But, my God, I was living . . .

He took me to dinner, wooed me, charmed me all over again. He vowed that it had only been a temporary lapse. But it wasn't. It heralded another bout of drinking. Another rainy day was here again.

Eleven

This time the drinking began gradually. He was still having meetings about the new series and the shows were rapidly becoming a reality. But, no matter what was happening professionally, at home, drunk or sober, he was in charge or thought himself to be. He certainly held the purse strings. Nevertheless I was learning how to handle him; however much things were falling apart outside, at home he needed to have his confidence restored and his ego stoked. There were large parts of him still submerged. Had I been the person I am now I would have dug for the truth, been stronger, helped him and brought these things to the surface. One of John's favourite speeches from a J. B. Priestley play was 'When I was no longer a boy I knew what sort of boy I ought to have been. By the time we are forty we know how to behave at twenty, but always too late.' I was thirty-five and in love for the first time in my life. I believed that love moved mountains, but I couldn't save Tony. Perhaps I made things worse. What I thought was love then is only a pale shadow of what I now know it to be. However, under all my foolishness I hung on to him. Looking back, I know to my shame that I didn't hang on hard enough.

One Friday lunchtime Tony rushed home from one of his meetings, obviously having passed a bar or two on the way. His eyes were shining. 'We're going to Paris,' he declared.

'When?'

'Now, this minute.'

'I'm cooking lunch,' I objected.

'Then switch it off. Come on. The car's waiting downstairs. Get your passport.'

I was dragged protesting out of the flat. 'I haven't got any make-up on or done any packing.'

'We'll buy it all there,' he said. 'I'll take you to Balmain's.'

The next thing I knew I was in the car with a ladder in my tights, had literally been dragged out of the house still wearing my apron, which I tore off at the last moment.

It wasn't boring being with Tony. Frightening? Yes. Exasperating? Yes. But never boring. Of course it was exciting going to Paris for the first time with my lover. But I would have liked to have gone properly, packed, prepared and looking good. My good nature fought my apprehension.

'You've got a little muscle that appears on the side of your mouth when you're trying not to be angry,' he said.

Apprehension fled.

In returned at the airport. While getting out of the car I caught the heel of my shoe in my hem. The hem drooped; I felt scruffy and plain.

A journalist spotted Tony. 'What are you going to Paris for, Mr Hancock?'

'Shopping,' said Tony grandly, making for the VIP lounge. This from the benefactor who once gave me a blank cheque to go to Marks and Spencer's to buy myself some underwear and, when he heard how much I'd spent, said, 'I'm not made of money, you know.' Now I was going to be dressed by Balmain?

In the first-class cabin, over a bottle of champagne, he asked a dignified black gentleman sitting opposite what the tribal scars on his face represented. Not best pleased, the gentleman told him. Tony looked at me and probably saw the anger muscle working furiously. 'Well,' he said defensively, 'how can you find out about things if you don't ask?'

Later Tony leaned over to a man on the other side of the aisle who kept smiling at him. 'Excuse me, but are you as big a prick as you look?' he asked good-naturedly. Fortunately the man roared with laughter. He turned out to be a well-known disc jockey, a fan.

I stared out of the window, wishing the plane would crash and put me out of my misery. Tony filled in our landing cards; I was listed as a Polish sheet-metal worker, he as an Ethiopian ballroom dancer.

While we were filing through passport control, Tony holding the landing cards and chuckling away, the disc jockey offered us a lift to Paris. He had a limousine waiting – more hospitality *en route*. He dropped us off at the hotel, which was situated somewhere on the Left Bank. We checked in and without even going to our room Tony ordered a taxi to take us sightseeing. He was in a fever to show me his beloved Paris. I just wanted a safety-pin for my hem, a new pair of tights, a bath and some mascara. 'You look lovely,' said Tony.

I was pulled out of the car in Montmartre, run around a square and into a bar, out again for another drink at the Georges V Hotel. The ladder in my tights widened. I felt bedraggled, sluttish and bewildered, not to mention hungry. Tears were not far away. Tony became exasperated. 'I bring you to Paris to give you a treat and this is the thanks I get!' he said in disgust.

'I'm hungry,' I said, and burst into tears.

He was immediately concerned and loving. 'Come on then,' he said. 'I'll take you somewhere nice.'

Somewhere nice was a brasserie on the corner of the square near the hotel. I hated it – it looked like a snack bar to me, all neon lights and chrome. I had hoped for somewhere candlelit and dark to hide my shabbiness.

Tony ordered for me – pork and mashed potatoes. The pork was fatty. My chin quivered.

'Fucking women,' he said, turning away from the table and putting his elbow into a huge apricot flan lying on the bar behind him. The look of surprise on his face broke my mood and I started to laugh. The waiter was not impressed. It made us worse. Tony paid for the flan, and we passed the rest of the meal, under the baleful eyes of the staff, in giggles. I helped Tony with the wine, which, with the love I felt for this clown, flowed through my veins. Together we floated home to bed, his sticky arm around me . . . God was in his heaven.

I didn't get to Balmain's. The next day I fixed my hem and managed to buy some make-up. Tony had his sleeve cleaned and we set off for some sightseeing.

We went for lunch at what seemed to me to be a transport café. I realize now that it was a well-known restaurant, but then I was unworldly about these things. As usual Tony ordered for me. 'What is it?' I asked as the food was put before me.

'Wild boar,' he replied.

'I don't want it,' I said vehemently.

'Eat it,' he commanded, his eyes cold, angry and grey.

I forced some down, my eyes brimming. It was delicious. His eyes turned blue again. The moment was saved.

During the afternoon we walked arm in arm around that beautiful city, Tony pointing out landmarks. I was enchanted by it. After a rest at the hotel he took me to dinner at Le Roi de Coquillage, a seafood restaurant. There were waiters wearing straw hats and white aprons and outside on the pavement a long bar containing every kind of shellfish – oysters, mussels, crabs, sea urchins . . . Tony ordered bouillabaisse to start. It was prepared at the table – every sort of fish imaginable in a huge tureen, with croutons piled with aïoli, a strong, garlicky mayonnaise, floating on top. With it we had dry white wine. Then came a wedding-cake-shaped tier of crushed ice piled with every kind of seafood. I ate sea urchins and oysters for the first time. It was wonderful. I was happy. This was Paris all right.

After dinner Tony ordered Russian vodka, very strong and neat, with our black coffee. When I returned from the ladies' room he had negotiated the purchase of a bottle.

'We don't need that, Tony,' I said.

'We'll just have one before bedtime at the hotel,' he said firmly.

On the way home I tried to work out how to get the bottle off him. He had several swigs of it in the taxi and began to maul me clumsily. In the bedroom he became rough and wanted to beat me. My nerve went. I rushed to the bathroom and threw up. Hearing me in distress, he calmed down, and we went to bed, but when I woke up the next morning he had already started on the bottle again. He had become a black, evil stranger.

I got dressed. He leaned back against the bedhead glaring at me, holding on to his precious bottle like a baby in case I tried to take the poisonous stuff away from him. Indeed, I would have had I been sure he wouldn't do me physical harm.

'Come on, Tony,' I urged, 'let's go out and look at Paris. We're in the most beautiful city in the world and here we are in this depressing bedroom.' But there was no budging him from that damned bottle.

'You go out. Go on, piss off and leave me alone,' he said.

This I did, after extracting a little money from him, which he gave grudgingly to get rid of me. I walked around the block wondering how I could extricate myself from this nightmare. Was it really less than forty-eight hours ago that I had been happily cooking lunch for him at home? It seemed like an eternity, another world. I wanted to get him safely back to London where the doctor could take care of him.

I had no money of my own, I felt lost and frightened alone in a strange city where I couldn't even speak the language. I would just have to sit it out with him and hope that he would come to his senses and take me home. I remembered Lily saying, 'Don't let him take you to Paris. He always behaved badly when he took his other wives there.' Why hadn't I resisted him? But how could anyone resist him when he was on a high like that?

I went into a book shop, saw a *Playboy* magazine, the

only English reading material I recognized, and bought it. By the time I got back he had acquired another bottle.

'Who have you been with?' was his greeting.

'Only a couple of men,' I quipped. 'I've been trying to earn my fare home. Please let's go home,' I pleaded.

'You go,' he said, 'you ungrateful bitch . . . Go on, get out!'

I wanted to with all my heart. I thought of my gentle, loving husband, my family and friends, and I wanted to run like the wind away from this monster, back to the safety of home. If only they could see what I had come to, what would they think?

I sat on a chair in the corner of the room and got out the *Playboy*.

'Don't read that shit in my presence,' Tony said. 'You illiterate cow!' He snatched it from me and threw it against the wall. I picked it up. He grabbed it from me and threw it at the wall again.

'I've got to do something while you're drinking yourself to death,' I said. 'I certainly can't bear to look at you.'

'Then go home. Go on, get back to your darling John. Go home and be safe.' So saying, he slung the air ticket at me.

'I need the taxi fare,' I said. 'I haven't got any money.' Tears of self-pity were running down my face now, but this time he was too far gone to give a damn. He was completely obsessed, completely evil.

I gathered up my few belongings and my ticket and headed for the door. Was this how our great romance would end? Could I really leave my lover alone in Paris to drink himself blind? What would people think of me? Supposing he died here?

I turned and looked at him sitting there guzzling from that bloody bottle, not even aware of what he was putting me through, and suddenly I wanted to kill him. My finger-nails seemed to grow into claws and I vaguely remember running at him, wanting to tear him to shreds, to tear that evil look off his face . . . And that is what I did. I seemed to

145

have the strength of ten. I grabbed the bottle, threw it at the wall and hit him. I punched him and scratched him like a wild beast. I drew blood and cursed him for all that he had done to me, sobbing and beating him with all my strength. It brought him to his senses. I think for the first time in our relationship I scared him. I was totally out of control and it got through to his drink-sodden brain that I had murder in my heart and was desperate.

Suddenly he was sober. 'All right, all right. Calm down. I'm sorry,' he kept saying. 'I'm sorry.' He pinned my arms to my sides and held on to me till the mists cleared and I surfaced out of the red haze. Shaking with sobs, I looked around at the room and his blood-spattered face. Never before or since have I lost control to that extreme. It scared me to death. I really think that I might have killed him. 'John Le Mesurier's wife murders Tony Hancock in a sleazy Paris hotel.' I could see it all pass before my eyes. What a story for the papers! What an ending to our great romance!

It took a while for me to calm down and stop gibbering and shaking. Tony was in command now and I was the invalid. He wiped my face. He looked a mess: one eye was closing rapidly and there was blood over the sheets; it was even splattered on the wall behind the bed. It looked as if a murder had taken place. I could only sit there dumb with horror at what I had done, my face puffed with tears and strain and his scratched and bruised.

Tony made a phone call and booked us on a flight back to England. So home we came from our romantic week-end in Paris, he sporting the biggest shiner I have ever seen. I ashen-faced and looking out through swollen eyelids. Tony bought us each a pair of dark glasses at the airport. In the plane we took them off and looked at each other. 'You look like Wallace Beery,' I said. Would you believe, we laughed all the way home.

After that Tony went on a tapering-off cure. Each morning when he awoke he shook with delirium tremens so badly that he was incapable of even turning the handle of the bathroom door. On the doctor's orders I had to measure out two ounces of alcohol diluted with water and feed it to him sip by sip because he couldn't hold the glass in his shaking hands.

I had to conceal some booze in the apartment. The hiding place was changed every day in case he discovered it. Mary, our cleaning lady, would bring in the drink secretly and we found ingenious ways of disguising its whereabouts. Once I put it in a hot-water bottle, but he tested the rubber when I gave him his 'medicine' and found the hiding place. In the middle of the night, even when drugged by the barbiturates he had to take to get to sleep, he would get up and stagger about searching for it. Once, while I slept, he slipped in the bathroom and cracked his head on the bidet. Only after the foul stuff had been consumed would he begin to function. The shakes would die away and his eyes would clear. He would spend the rest of the day trying to control his longing for more. They were long, long days. It seemed a strange sort of treatment, but without it he would have gone into withdrawal, the shock of which might have resulted in another dreadful epileptic-type fit.

Somehow he got straight again and managed to record the new series of television shows. There were problems, but he didn't want to discuss them. I never went with him on the nights the shows were recorded – he didn't want me there and I didn't want to be there. I hated his work and longed for him to give it up. It was my rival and the tensions it contained always drove him back to the bottle. I was a selfish little bitch in that respect. I was no help at all to him professionally, as Freddie had been. She had striven valiantly to put him back on top; I made jokes about his investing in a blowlamp and taking up plumbing. All I wanted was Tony, far away from public life. I had this dream of us living quietly in the country pottering about in the garden. Fat chance I had.

In July 1967 Tony was asked to go to Aden with Hughie

Green to entertain the troops during the troubles there; afterwards he was to go to Hong Kong where he was booked to do a cabaret act for a month. Grudgingly and jealously I relinquished him. I spent the time with David, who moved in with me for company. Together we combed the shops trying to find finishing touches for the flat. By then I had been given the huge amount of £15 a week and credit cards for the big stores. I was a trustee.

Tony rang up regularly from Hong Kong. He met Anne Shelton there and she became his confidante. I met her after Tony's death while she was doing cabaret in Ramsgate and we became firm friends. When she discovered I had been Tony's lady she burst into tears. She said he would go on for hours about me, but he never told her who I was, just that he was very much in love.

During the calls I detected that he was drinking. He was very adept at hiding the fact but by then I knew the signs. He asked me what I would like him to bring back as a souvenir and, getting my cultures mixed, I asked for a kimono.

At last the telegram arrived. I still have it, tattered and frayed: 'Can't wait to get home. Meet me at Heathrow.'

He came through the doors of the arrival lounge laughing with pleasure and booze, holding out his arms. The promised kimono had changed into an eight-foot-tall teddy bear and a watch. The former needed two men to carry it to the waiting limousine. There was also a bill from the customs men for £50. On the bear's foot was a small sign: 'Made in England.'

We propped the bear against the living-room wall; it was so big that we could both sit between its legs. If only I'd had a camera – I have him photographed on my heart, though, leaning back against the bear's massive chest, talking to me while I gazed fondly at them both.

The bear brought a solid comfortable presence into our home and we used him as an intermediary during arguments. 'Tell her to pull herself together, for fuck's sake,' Tony would say to it. 'Tell your friend to get stuffed,' I would reply.

Eventually the bear took up the violin. I don't know how, but the bear suddenly acquired one and sat there with it tucked under its chin. 'He was playing "The Flight of the Bumble Bee" all bloody night again,' Tony would say. In a book about him, written just after his death, Freddie Ross mentioned that Tony had a weird habit of talking to stuffed toys. I found it funny and engaging, but then *I* was as crazy as he was.

His show was not well received when it was broadcast at the end of July. The response upset him and served as an excuse for another bout of heavy drinking. He disappeared one day while on his way home after a meeting at Delfont's – no doubt something had upset him. I waited at home for three days during which he phoned a couple of times. He had fallen into a ditch, he told me laughingly before he hung up, leaving me frustrated, angry and fearful.

At about five o'clock on the fourth day the intercom rang and I heard Tony talking to the porter. By the tone of their respective voices I knew what I was going to see. The porter sounded solicitous and concerned, Tony blurred and defiant.

I waited at the front door. The lift opened. Tony was grinning cheekily, his tie on back to front; his trousers, which had slipped down low on his hips, bagged out over his shoes. His chin was covered in stubble, his eyes were bloodshot, he stank, and he was holding out his arms for a welcome-home kiss. I tied a knot in my heart and side-stepped his lurching embrace. Once inside the flat I said, 'I'm phoning the doctor to come and take care of you and then I'm off. I've had it this time.'

'You'd be proud of me if you knew what I've been doing,' he said, hurt and misunderstood.

'What was that, Tony?' I asked patiently.

'I've been helping a sick friend,' he slurred.

I gave a shudder of disgust and rang the doctor. Tony

dropped to his knees, pulling out all the stops. He implored; he begged. In desperation he came up with, 'The reason I drink is because you're more intelligent than I am and it makes me feel inadequate.'

'Nice try, Tony,' I said, biting my lip, 'but it's too late. I'm at the end of my tether.'

By the time the doctor arrived Tony had gone through the whole repertoire, from flattery to begging. I left him with the doctor and went to prepare a bath, knowing I would never leave him, but determined to get my revenge and put the fear of God into him before I succumbed once again.

The doctor said that it was impossible to sedate him while he was full of booze and suggested that I should let him take me out to dinner to placate me; in the morning he could begin the tapering-off treatment once again. Tony readily agreed, supported between the bear's paws and trying to look boyish, while I paced the room, enjoying my moment of power over him and airing my complaints. Eventually I agreed to stay and Tony gratefully lurched towards me for his belated kiss.

'You stink,' I said. 'Go and bathe while I make some tea.'

While the doctor and I were in the kitchen we heard an almighty splash. We put our heads around the door to see Tony sitting in the bath, fully clothed, with his legs hooked over the side. He had fallen backwards into the tub while trying to clean his teeth, the tube of toothpaste in one hand, the brush in the other. 'Good mornings,' he said, 'always begin with Signal, the toothpaste with the mouth-wash in the stripes.'

A few hours later a repentant, scrubbed and bleary Tony took me to dinner at the Coq Hardi whence I refused to be seduced until I had eaten a hearty meal.

The second disappearance a few weeks later had more serious and far-reaching consequences. Tony was gone for four days again and this time I waited without a phone call or a sign from him. When he finally arrived home, preceded by six dozen long-stem red roses and accompanied by his driver, he was the worse for wear, much more so than on the previous occasion. The demon in him wasn't far below the surface this time. He kept grabbing me and mouthing obscenities.

'Why did you let him get like this?' I shouted at the driver while struggling to escape from Tony's advances.

'I work for Mr Hancock,' he replied. 'I do as I'm told.'

'You're helping him destroy himself,' I yelled, and I ran from the room, leaving the two of them over a bottle, good friends ranged against me. I went into the bedroom. Mentally and physically exhausted, I was dreading the state he'd be in when he eventually came to bed.

I was sorting out Tony's sleeping pills, which I kept hidden in a sewing basket, when I suddenly had an overwhelming desire to sleep, to escape, to get away from Tony and the situation. On impulse I shook a number of pills into my hand and swallowed them, reasoning with what was left of my brain that the amount I had taken wouldn't kill me but would give me some peace.

I remember hiding the bottle under the mattress and then drifting quite swiftly into a deep, quiet oblivion. Later, through the pill-induced haze, I remember being pulled by my hair off the bed and on to the floor, where the monster that was Tony gruntingly tried to make love to me. He lurched away and I recall thinking, 'I'm still in the nightmare.' I climbed back on to the bed, searched for and found the bottle of pills. How many more I took I'll never know.

My next recollection was hearing a voice, far away, imploring me to think of my son, and then the doctor's voice. My face was slapped, there was a pain in my arm (an injection to bring me round), then I was lifted and dragged to my feet and told to walk. My legs wouldn't respond. All the time there were voices, slaps, arms holding me up, coffee being forced down my throat, rough treatment, and the overwhelming desire to be left alone to sleep.

I woke up in a cot in a hospital ward, shouting that I

wanted to shit. A bedpan was produced, which I refused. I wanted to use a lavatory and attempted to climb over the bars of the cot. I was wheeled, still shouting (I can't remember what), out of the ward, where I was placed on a lavatory. I was wearing a hospital gown with ties at the back. Two nurses stood by while I relieved myself, yelling at them to leave me alone. Then it was morning and a young doctor was standing by my bed talking sternly about having me certified. 'Put me away, *please*. Lock me away somewhere where I'll be safe,' I implored. I was still shouting belligerently, unaware of the other poor patients. Something had happened to my brain – my conduct was appalling.

A good friend, Wendy Riches, arrived. She had come to take me home with her and I was discharged into her care. Wendy is one of my friends whom I actually *acquired* during my affair with Tony. She worked on a BBC children's programme, training birds and animals for the show. She has an amazing knack with all creatures, being able to tame and handle even the most savage. She has the same effect on people. She is the kindest person it has ever been my good luck to encounter.

Her house and small garden in Putney contained a strange selection of animals being trained for the show. Anong her private menagerie was an old cockatoo called Goofy. He had belonged to her grandfather and was an old trouper, having been on the boards for many years. He would do a dance on the table to 'Pop Goes the Weasel', but if you laughed at him he would fly into a rage, put his head down and charge at your nose. I was enchanted by him: he was the only thing that cheered me up at that time, and while I was recovering Wendy would put him on my bed so he could do his act for me.

I stayed at Wendy's for five days and, while there, tried to piece together the recent shameful happenings. Tony was in a nursing home taking another cure. He had been forbidden by his psychiatrist to have any contact with me. I was told that I had done him irreparable harm by behaving as Freddie had done and my calls to him were not put through.

So here I was in another fine pickle. I'd narrowly escaped death, I was too ill to look after myself and having to be cared for by Wendy, my love was locked up and I couldn't get in touch with him, and I didn't even have my own clothes with me and there was no way of getting them. How love can bring us to our knees and literally strip us bare.

Twelve

Dorothy Squires came to get me, I don't know how she found out about what had happened. Perhaps Wendy had phoned her, I certainly hadn't told anybody. The last thing I wanted was that John or my family should find out about the mess I was in.

Dorothy wanted to deliver me back into the care of my family. She knew how worried and unhappy they all were and thought that this would be as good a time as any, when I was flat on my back.

She was harsh but kind. 'Is this what love has done for you, my girl?' she said, holding a mirror in front of me. 'Have a look at yourself.'

I had to admit that I had looked better. I had aged ten years. My face had taken the strain all right. Every horrendous experience over the past year must have added another line.

'I'm taking you home with me,' said Dorothy. 'Don't tell anyone where she is until I've got her on her feet again,' she said to Wendy. Then she dressed me, wrapped her mink coat around me, bundled me into her car and drove me down to her house in Bexley.

When we arrived she gave me a stern talking to, reminding me how happy I had been before all this had happened, promising me that, if only I had the strength to stay away from Tony, I would recover from this hopeless infatuation. She pointed out how many people were suffering because of me and what a fortunate woman I was to be blessed with a husband as patient and understanding as John. She ended by saying that she understood how I felt about Tony. 'But it's too late. You can't do anything for him. You can only destroy yourself. You nearly did, and think what that would have done to the people who love you. You must think about David now and put Tony out of your mind.'

There was no disputing the truth of what she said. I had tried hard, and time and time again Tony had let me down. I went cold with horror at the thought of how near I had been to my own destruction. I promised her that when I had got my strength back I would go back to John and try to make amends. 'But how I'm going to cope, knowing Tony's lonely and sick somewhere I just don't know.' The tears began again at the thought of it.

'You must harden your heart. You'll want to phone him a hundred times a day, but you musn't,' Dorothy said sympathetically. 'And it *will* get easier.' She made me take some sleeping pills and put me to bed, where I slept like the dead until four the next afternoon, when she woke me with a tray of food.

Tony had rung her several times while I'd been asleep. He had tried everyone who knew me, and though Dorothy protested that she had no idea where I was, she suspected he didn't believe her. She was worried that he might turn up in Bexley.

The thought that Tony was looking for me and was desperate filled me with the urge to rush to the phone and tell him where I was. I had a terrible feeling that I wouldn't be strong enough not to. If I saw him, how would I be able to resist him? In spite of everything that had happened, I wanted nothing more than to be with him. It was as if he'd got inside me and was willing me back to him. I explained this to Dorothy, but again she argued that as I became stronger and if I stayed away from him long enough, I would be able to cope.

The phone rang that evening. It was Tony again. This time Dorothy put on a thick Welsh accent and pretended to be the maid. 'Dorothy's gone away,' she said. 'No, I don't know where. She'll be away quite some time.' When she'd hung up, she said, 'He's suspicious. I don't think he swallowed that. We've got to get away from here.' She made a phone call. 'We're going to Brighton. I've got some friends there.'

Within the hour we were on our way. She had hurriedly sorted out something for me to wear and packed a few things for herself, determined to protect me from myself at all costs.

Dorothy's friends lived in a beautiful Regency house near the seafront. They were a wealthy young gay couple and they made me welcome. Dorothy told them nothing about me except that I was on the run from a complicated affair. After a few days' rest and some long walks in the fresh air I began to feel stronger. Dorothy was kindness itself and stayed with me, trying to keep my spirits up, looking forward to delivering me back to John.

On the Saturday night the boys gave a dinner party for a few friends. One of them, a woman whose name I can't recall, sat next to me at dinner and we fell into a deep conversation. She was a widow, recently bereaved after a long and happy marriage. Before long I found myself telling her my story. She was all sympathy, softened by her recent loss. When I finished she said, 'All I know is that where there's life, there's hope.' Then she said something that I'd been waiting to hear. 'If your man had an incurable illness, would you give him up?'

'Of course not,' I replied.

'Isn't alcoholism an incurable illness, and often fatal?'

'You're absolutely right,' I said. There was no argument and I wanted none. The whole world could turn against me, but one person pleading his cause was all I needed. I excused myself and went to the phone.

When he heard my voice he said, 'Thank God. I'd almost given up. There was nothing left to do but wait here by the phone and pray. Will you come back to me?'

'Yes, I will,' I said.

'When?'

'Tomorrow.'

'No, that won't do. I've got to see you now. Where are you?

'I'm in Brighton.'

'I'm coming to get you right now. Give me the address and telephone number. I'll be there in an hour.'

He arrived soon after. He was wearing a thin stage suit, the first thing to hand after he had put the phone down. He had apparently walked into the street and flagged down the first taxi he saw and offered the driver £50 to take him to Brighton. He didn't have a penny in his pocket, let alone a cheque book.

Shivering with cold in his thin suit, his face alight with pleasure, he walked straight past my hosts and seized me. 'Come on then, are you ready?' he said like an excited schoolboy, wanting only to be alone.

'Please don't rush off,' said the boys, disappointed at losing him as soon as he'd arrived.

'Can't stay,' said Tony, staring into my eyes. 'I haven't any money to pay the taxi. We've got to get back.'

The boys lent him the money for the fare and persuaded him to stay the night. After charming a defeated Dorothy with a hug, he excused us and took me off to bed.

The next morning he borrowed a black fur jacket from one of the boys, leaving his expensive watch as surety for that, and the £50, and we went for a walk on the promenade. He swanked about in the jacket, which looked as if it was made for him. I told him my suspicions about the driver. Tony told me that Freddie's repeated suicide attempts had prevented him from taking any of my behaviour seriously.

In the condition he must have been in, he would have been incapable of knowing what was really going on anyway. His psychiatrist had done his best to persuade him to end our relationship, convinced that I was using emotional blackmail. But neither he nor Dorothy had been able to separate us. So there we were back together, with me prepared to believe his promises, anything he said, rather than be without him.

Dorothy drove us back to Bexley that night. At one point, while we were sitting together in her study, Tony and I trying to convince her that all would be well, she broke down and sobbed, knowing that our relationship was doomed, but unable to help any more. I've never forgotten her tears. It was the only time I ever saw her cry. She is a very tough lady, but I know that her sorrow was genuine and I'll never forget her kindness.

The fight against booze was becoming harder, the moments of calm between each bout shorter. Tony was a sick man, his illness more apparent during his periods of sobriety than when he was blurred by drink. Things were rapidly falling apart now, the bad reviews he had received for *Hancock's* were yet another worm in the apple of his self-confidence. Plans were made and scrapped, laid by his legend, laid aside by the fainthearted. He was pushing me to the limits now. Testing, testing.

My love for him was as strong as ever but I was losing my faith. I had really believed that love moved mountains and conquered all, but it couldn't conquer this death wish. The side of him that came to the surface when he drank was growing more alien, blacker and humourless. I was becoming frightened of it, sick of trying to coax and wheedle him away from the next drink.

There were no more dry-outs, only half-hearted attempts to reduce his intake. Once more the subterfuge of hiding bottles from him began. He promised not to drink at home, apart from the heart-starter to stop the morning shakes. Our social life widened simply because he was chasing a drink. It wasn't all bad – there were the good times still dotted about under the cloud of his unpredictability. From time to time I was taken out, to a good restaurant and to the theatre.

Lily had a friend, an admirer. A millionaire no less, he was the owner of a Silver Cloud Rolls-Royce and would occasionally bring Lily to London in it, where they would stay at the Savoy Hotel. He was a 'gentleman', and Lily was on tenterhooks that Tony would go too far in his company and show her up, so meetings between her friend George and Tony were usually brief.

On one occasion George invited us to the theatre during one of their weekends in town. We accepted, Tony promised Lily that the drinking would be minimal.

The show was *Charlie Girl*, and we arranged to meet them in the Savoy Bar for tea, as we were going to the Saturday matinée. Afterwards we were to dine at the Garden Restaurant in Covent Garden, as George's guest. The matinée was Lily's idea; she thought that a pre-theatre tea would be safer than pre-theatre cocktails.

George, knowing nothing of Tony's problem, innocently offered Tony something a little stronger to go with the set tea, and by the time we arrived at the theatre Tony was in good spirits, inside and out. As we walked down the centre aisle he was mobbed by autograph hunters, and by the time we got to our seats he was puffed by praise and adoration.

Not long into the show, after Anna Neagle's first number, Tony said in a stage whisper, 'You'd think she'd know how to use a mike after all these years, wouldn't you?' A little later on, he hissed, 'I think one of the usherettes is on the lighting.' He was shushed by the man sitting in front of him. 'Who are you, then?' said Tony in the man's ear. 'One of Herbert Wilcox's relatives.'

'Will you be quiet?' hissed the man.

'Stone me, I can't hear a thing,' said Tony, completely ignoring the man. 'What's happened to the mike? I could hear a sparrow fart in this auditorium. I mean, am I right in thinking that I'm in the West End?'

By the time the interval came Lily was in a state of collapse. Nervous as I was about the outcome. I was having a hard time to keep from laughing.

On the way to the bar I whispered to Lily that I didn't think it a good idea to go back for the second half under the circumstances. She agreed, saying that wild horses wouldn't get her to go through that again and that we had better try to get him out of the theatre after the interval.

In the bar Tony met up with a party of lady publicans on an outing. 'This is Beryl from the Lord Nelson, Penge,' he said, wiping his eyes, 'and Doris of the Dog and Duck, oh dear!' He was off, in hysterics.

The ladies bore him to the bar and plied him with drinks. It was right up his street, and mine too had I not been only too aware of poor Lily's discomfort in the presence of George, who was, however, taking the whole thing in good part. 'I'll never forgive him for this, never,' Lily whispered to me as we watched Tony at the bar, surrounded by jolly ladies, roaring with laughter at each new introduction and oblivious to Lily's set face.

'Here, come here,' he gestured to me from among the throng. 'Now, tell my friend here where you're from,' he said to yet another. 'Maud from The Star and Garter, Folkestone and Madge from the Blazing Donkey in Eastry.'

The whole incident was designed to put him in the best of spirits, and as we left the theatre I begged Lily to go along with it so as not to change his jovial mood. There was always a shadow underlying all the laughter, the fear of the lurking monster who waited just below the surface for him to be rubbed up the wrong way, and who appeared, like the evil genie, out of a bottle.

In the Garden Restaurant all was affability and laughter. Tony was, however, becoming increasingly loud and at one point, Lily, in spite of her intent to humour him, said, 'Tony, do keep your voice down.' Thereupon two ladies at the next table leaned over and said. 'Don't tell him off, he's lovely.' Needing no invitation and wanting to be where the praise was, Tony joined them.

'I can't take any more of this,' said poor Lily, her hopes that Tony wouldn't disgrace her having been sadly dashed. George paid the bill and as they left Tony jovially waved them off, while I, still in his good books, managed to get him home without any unpleasantness occurring.

The next time we ventured out, it was to see *Who's*

Afraid of Virginia Woolf which he enjoyed. However, something in the story was too close to home – the antagonism and the sordid drinking. When we arrived home he started analysing the plot, finding similarities in our situation. In truth, he was spoiling for a fight. By the end of the night I was barricaded in the study, while Tony, maddened with rage and shouting obscenities, hammered on the door.

In the early morning when he had fallen silent I crept out, terrified that he would waken and do me harm. Grabbing my bag and coat, I let myself out of the flat and went round to Marion. 'This time,' I vowed, 'I'm not going back.'

Two days later Marion and I were on the top of a bus coming from Kensington High Street. As we passed the flat I saw Tony making his way across the road on his way to the off licence. He was unshaven and staggering. I jumped up. A lot of people on the bus had seen him too.

Marion tried to pull me back on to the seat. 'Don't look,' she said.

I got off the bus at the traffic lights and caught him coming out of the shop. 'You look well,' I said sarcastically, not knowing how I would be received, but wanting to get him off the street.

'Where've you been?' he said in a slurred voice, grinning happily.

'Just shopping,' I said. 'Let's go home.' He allowed me to lead him away.

But it happened again. I was beginning to turn up on Marion's doorstep with increasing regularity. He came round to get me a couple of times. Once I went to Ramsgate and he phoned me there. He spoke to my father, drunkenly telling him to send me back. He knew that he was destroying our chances of a future, that my endurance was failing, but he was powerless to stop.

One day, when I had managed to talk to him honestly about what was happening, ending by telling him tearfully that he was closing the door on me and begging him to stop before it was too late, I seemed to get through and, full of contrition, he made the usual promises. Later that day he expressed a wish to talk to my father. He needed cheering up and Dad could usually be counted on to make him laugh. I dialled the number while Tony, smiling expectantly, waited for me to pass the phone to him. But before I could speak Dad said, 'Your mother and I have decided that we never want that man in our house again.' I tried to get a word in, but he went on, 'We know what you feel, but he's disrupted our lives long enough and we can't put up with any more.' He ended with, 'Your mother's a nervous wreck, crying all the time. So we're washing our hands of him.'

There was nothing to say. I put down the phone.

The smile on Tony's face faded. 'What have I done?' he said. 'I'm ruining your life.'

'Our life,' I said.

I firmly believe that the good in him was fighting the bad for its life in those last weeks. It was as if his personality was split in two and in his weakened state the evil side was gaining strength.

We experienced a path of calm after that talk and my parents' rejection. One evening he took me to The Royal Garden Hotel again. It was a peace offering and we set off in high spirits.

The food and the wine were delicious, and so was he – he was at his most lovable and sexy. There was a band and people were dancing, not a thing Tony was inclined to do, but we enjoyed watching the others. Suddenly, without any warning, from both sides of the stage the room filled with violinists. They were playing 'The Flight of the Bumble Bee', obviously having been tipped off that Tony was there. They made a 'Bumble Bee' line to our table and surrounded us, sawing furiously and grinning.

'Take me to your leader,' said Tony, and he slowly disappeared under the table, helpless with laughter. It crowned the evening for us and we laughed all the way home.

He was in such a good mood that just before we arrived at the flat, he suddenly changed his mind about going in. 'It's early yet, and you're all dressed up,' he said. 'Come on, I'm taking you up west for a nightcap.'

The smile left my face. 'Nightcap' meant more booze – he had only drunk wine that evening and all had been well until then.

'Couldn't we go in, Tony?' I asked him. 'It's been so lovely, let's not spoil it.'

His face darkened. 'What do you mean, spoil it? I'm offering to take you somewhere nice and you say "Let's not spoil it."' He imitated my voice. He banged on the dividing window of the taxi and instructed the driver to take us to the Stork Club.

The happy mood had disappeared. At the club he drank several brandies and grew increasingly hostile. Whatever I said was received with argument, until I fell silent, dreading the moment when we would be alone.

Back at the flat, while I prepared for bed, he glowered at me, and when I turned the bedcovers down he said, 'I don't want you to sleep with me tonight.'

I froze. 'Then I'll sleep in the study,' I said, trying to keep the fear and hostility out of my voice.

'I think you should go right away from me for your good, because there's some part of me that is capable of harming you, even killing you.' His voice was cold, but he didn't sound drunk. I think that the part of him that was still intact was really warning me about the part that wasn't.

I was deathly afraid now and made the mistake of touching him.

'Don't touch me, you bitch,' he shouted, shaking off my hand.

I ran then, as fast as I could, to the safety of the study. I just had time to slide the bolt when the banging started on the other side of the door. Once more the furniture was piled against it making a barricade between me and the man I loved. I spent the night sitting shaking with fear, knowing that this time the game was up. It was over. I had lost him.

I got out safely. Whether he was asleep or whether he just let me go, I don't know. I went to Marion's as usual, and after a few weeks I went back to John, who welcomed me, lovingly and warmly, as if I had been on some heroic mission or had just come home from hospital after a long illness. No word of recrimination passed his lips and no questions were asked. He simply wanted the past year erased from our minds. He believed that if we didn't talk about them and bring them to the surface, the memories would evaporate and disappear.

Of course the memories didn't disappear. Tony was with me constantly, though I heard nothing from him, not a word, and I made no contact. My clothes were still in the flat and I left them there.

I forced myself to keep busy, determined to make it up to John for the wrongs of the past year. I decorated the flat, changing the whole look of the place, making it fresh and new, to match my new resolutions. I was determined to keep busy at all costs.

Some of my former friends, unable to be as magnanimous as John, cut me dead.

In early October I heard that Tony was in Australia. I heaved a sigh of relief, knowing that he was working and not sitting alone in his London flat, as he had been when he first came into my life. Now there was no danger of my seeing him when I passed our old flat. I looked up at the windows every time, as I still do to this day, out of habit.

My sigh of relief was short-lived, changed to one of despair when I read in the newspapers a few days later that he had gone on stage hopelessly drunk during a cabaret performance in a Melbourne theatre. He had fallen down several times, used foul language and crashed off the stage, crawling back on his hands and knees, before the management halted the show. Apparently some idiot had laced his tomato juice with vodka at a drinks party before he went on. He had been dry until then. The alcohol, combined with the drugs he needed when he was dry, had been a fatal mixture, resulting in his public disgrace. Poor Tony, what he must have suffered after that. Even so when he went on the following night, his opening line 'As I was saying when I fell off the stage' brought the house down. All was forgiven by his faithful fans.

I was deeply disturbed by this news. He may have been on the other side of the world, but news of him brought back all my old feelings. His welfare was a constant source of concern. However, on the credit side, all was well at home. John was busy, plenty of work was coming in, and his life was in order once again. As for my parents, they were relieved that all was back to normal.

In early December I went to stay in Ramsgate. John was away doing location work and I was busy preparing for Christmas. We were planning to spend it with my family as usual. On this particular Saturday, while David and I were shopping for gifts in Canterbury an overwhelming feeling of excitement and anticipation came over me. It was so strong that I shuddered, as if a rabbit had walked over my grave.

On the television during the following afternoon there was a preview of that evening's chat show. I forget who the interviewer was, it was so long ago, but in the preview he announced that they were hoping to introduce a mystery guest. David and I were alone at the time, and I said to David, 'That's going to be Tony.'

David said, 'Mum, don't say I told you this, but I heard Nanny and Papa talking last night, and they said that Tony rang you yesterday and wanted to talk to you. And they told him that you were back with John and to leave you alone.'

This threw me into such a state of excitement and longing that I spent the rest of the day on tenterhooks. I had a hard time concealing my feelings. I was certain now that I would see Tony on the television that night and, sure enough, there he was.

He looked wonderful, full of confidence and right back

on form, describing his favourite *Come Dancing* programme, which we had seen and laughed at together so
many times. All his past sins were forgiven and I wanted
nothing more than to run out of the house and go to him.
No warning bells rang, common sense fled. I just wanted
to see him.

Fortunately I had already made plans to return to
London the next day. An unexpected departure would
have made my parents suspicious. As it was they were
worried by his appearing on the television.

'Forget him, old love,' my Dad said after the show.
'Think of John. He's been through enough, because of
Tony.' Straightfaced, I assured him that there was nothing
to worry about.

The next morning, after I had taken David to school, I
rang Tony from a call box. 'Hello,' I said. 'It's me.'

There was a long pause. 'Will you come back to me?' he
said.

'I'm coming to London today,' I told him.

'I'll meet the train,' he said, and we set a time.

He was waiting for me, hunched in the black fur coat. I
had trembled all the way from Ramsgate. We flung our
arms around each other and stood like that for a good
minute without speaking.

I felt like a junkie having my first fix after a long period
of self-control and denial.

He took me back to the flat and I stayed with him there
until the following morning, by which time I had told him
that there was no way back for us, I was not going to hurt
John again. We had had our chance and muffed it, and
there was no way out this time.

He knew the truth of this and accepted it. There was no
choice. We had to make do with what we had from then
on.

I promised I would spend every available moment of my
free time with him whenever possible, but John must not
suspect that I was seeing him again. It wasn't much of a
promise, but it was better than nothing.

'You'll come back to me one day,' he said. 'I don't know when or how, but I'm going to prove myself worthy by not letting you down again. And one day you're going to marry me.'

I went home happy, totally lacking any shadow of guilt and feeling complete again.

Thirteen

And so began the last chapter of our life together, this time conducted in secret. Only David was taken into my confidence. However, Marion guessed that I was seeing Tony again when she noticed a vase of blue flowers in the window of his living room. She knew that it was I who bought flowers for the house and that I always chose blue ones. Blue was my favourite colour, and his.

How we managed to see each other without being found out was a wonder. Most of the time John was working, and when he was at home it was possible at some point during the day to use the excuse of shopping or visiting friends. I became an expert in subterfuge, John making it easy for me because he never asked me where I'd been. He never asked a question if he didn't want to know the answer.

It was the hardest time of my whole life – I virtually ran two homes. Mary was a wonderful help, as was her husband. Her job extended far beyond cleaning the flat: she became housekeeper, cook, secretary and companion to Tony. Sometimes, when he was depressed, she and her husband would stay with him all night or take him home with them. He hated to be alone, especially at night; in the past he had been known to ask friends to share hotel rooms with him.

One day we met each other at Waterloo station after Tony had spent a weekend with Lily at Bournemouth. He took me to the Gore Hotel and over lunch he told me that he had taken a woman to Bournemouth for company – an actress whom he had met while filming the *Hancock's* series the previous April. She was just a friend, he said, and they had returned together on the same train. His confession took me by surprise because, up to then, it had never occurred to me that he might meet another woman. I believed that my only rivals were his fame and his drinking. I bit my lip throughout lunch, not sure of my feelings or if I believed him. In the whole time we had been together I had never experienced a pang of jealousy about Cicely or Freddie – even in the midst of all our problems and dramas, I was totally certain of his love for me.

By the time we arrived back at the apartment, however, I had become cold and remote. I asked him nonchalantly if the woman was married or had any domestic ties, and when he said no, I suggested that she should move in, adding how relieved I was that he had found someone to care for him. During this outburst he stood looking at me with a mocking smile which prompted me to further play-acting.

'Well, now all that's settled, I'll leave you and get back to John,' I said, and headed towards the door.

He grabbed me, holding me firmly by the arms, forcing me to look into his eyes. 'She's kind, and she keeps me company when you're not here,' he said. 'If it makes you unhappy I'll never see her again. You know that you have nothing to be jealous about and that I only want to be able to live with you. Come on, own up, you know you love me.'

And I did believe him – deep down, throughout it all, I knew that I was his only love.

Amazingly, when I got used to the idea, it was a relief to know that he wasn't alone at night half drugged and falling about or drunk and depressed.

Once, when, intentionally or out of curiosity, I stayed with him later than usual, she arrived at the door to take over the night shift. She was timid and shy, and she almost slunk into the living room as if she were being interviewed for a position. She wasn't pretty, but that isn't why, in the midst of all the strange feelings, jealousy was absent. She was self-effacing and obviously awed and besotted by Tony. At a loss to know how to behave with her or what to say in such a bizarre situation, I went back to the bedroom.

Tony was sitting on the bed in his familiar and beloved white robe, looking apprehensive and slightly sheepish.

'You do believe now that there is nothing to worry about, don't you?' he said.

I did, and told him so. As I left I put my head round the door of the living room and said, 'Isn't he a trial?' and she smiled nervously.

Once or twice after that, hurrying back to get John's dinner ready before he came home from work, I would pass her in the road and we'd stop and exchange a few pleasantries. What a strange existence it was.

Tony had told me that she slept on the day bed in the study, but one afternoon, after making love and in a state of post-coital bliss, I was looking for something in the bedside cupboard when I found a babydoll nightdress. I held it up, a film of blood swimming before my eyes. 'How did this get here?' I said in fury.

Tony, totally unprepared, was taken aback. 'I have no idea,' he blundered. 'She must have put it there.'

'After sleeping in our bed?' I said.

He blundered on. 'It's not like you imagine,' he said. 'Please understand. I swear I haven't made love to her.'

'I understand all right,' I yelled, and holding the accursed garment, I marched out of the room. In the kitchen I cut it into pieces. Back in the bedroom I flung the tattered bits of nightie at him, and he sat there, frills coyly framing his face, and tried to make me laugh.

But I wasn't having any of it this time. I dressed hurriedly, went to the phone and rang the poor woman (we had exchanged numbers in case of an emergency!). 'You can come over here and look after your lover,' I spat at her. 'I shan't be coming here any more.'

Tony snatched the phone from me and mumbled something about a misunderstanding, while I headed for the door fuming with jealous indignation. He ran after me, pleading with me to stay. 'It's nothing,' he called to my retreating back. 'Don't go.'

But I went, too incensed to realize how unreasonably I was behaving. After all, John and I had made love since I had returned to him. What if she *had* slept in his bed; what if they had made love even, which I still doubted. I knew that I had no rival in his heart. The truth was the strain was beginning to tell.

Having slept on it, I realized how unfairly I had behaved, whatever had happened between them. The most important thing was that Tony was trying harder these days – his drinking was under control and he was wooing me all over again, trying to win me back into his life, knowing that this time it would work only if his love for me was greater than his need for alcohol. I knew it was a tall order. But I also knew where his heart lay. It was the only certainty. The one fact that I knew for sure was that we belonged together. Being with him was as natural as breathing and if, as he often said, we had lived through other incarnations, we had known each other during them. There was a reason why we had met; there was something we had to work out together. I once quoted a line by Christopher Fry to him – 'God moved many lives to show you to me. It was complicated but very kind.' And so I rang him as soon as John left for work and asked his forgiveness, which he granted laughingly, and I hurried back to find him if anything slightly reassured, puffed up by my jealousy.

Then it was Christmas, the second time, and this time Tony went home to Lily and I went home to Ramsgate once more to the family. And still he was better, working hard at impressing me, at his most attractive and adult, and his most vulnerable.

I can't remember much about Christmas that year, only that it passed in a haze of subterfuge and deceit. Still, no one appeared to be suspicious – probably if my parents had any doubts they were prepared to keep quiet about them.

Tony's name didn't come up, only to my son David when we were alone and I gave him Tony's present, which we passed off as mine. Nevertheless, in the months since our reunion I had taken many liberties and risks. Any other man but John would have discovered what I was up to long before.

There had been one weekend just before Christmas when, after I had spent the afternoon with Tony before leaving for Ramsgate, where I was going to spend the weekend, having left John in London working on his lines, Tony was loathe to let me go. He decided to take me to the station, trying to persuade me all the while to risk it and stay with him. I refused, consumed as usual by maternal guilt. Guilt is and always has been a great shadow over my life, and even now all the logic and philosophizing can't quite erase it. As outrageous as my life has been, I have never embarked upon an adventure without a churning stomach and a lot of self-persuasion that 'Life is for living!'

So, after talking me into missing the first train, Tony took me to the Grosvenor Hotel bar, where we found a friend of mine and her boyfriend. They joined their voices to Tony's and in the face of their entreaties I stayed. I rang Ramsgate and told David where I was; to my parents I said that I was going to stay with a depressed girlfriend. The four of us had a jolly dinner together, and I enjoyed the luxury of three stolen nights in Tony's bed.

When I reluctantly returned home to John late on Monday afternoon, I knew that I had gone too far – he would have rung Ramsgate in my absence. In the lift I rehearsed my alibi. As I entered John was sitting by the telephone in the hall. 'I didn't go home for the weekend,' I said. 'I went to see Beau. I wanted to get away – I needed a change of scene.'

'But she's just phoned this very minute saying that she hasn't seen you for weeks,' said John gently, taking the ground from under my feet.

I thought quickly, came up with, 'She's a liar,' and swept into the bedroom.

No more was said – no questions asked – no explanations given. That's the sort of man I was married to: he had the ability to stick his head firmly in the sand and keep it there until the danger had passed. So we lumbered on.

Early in 1968 Tony was invited to do a television series in Australia. It was a great opportunity for him to make a comeback. He was adored out there; his *Hancock's Half Hour* series was currently being shown on television and he was in great demand. The fact that the series had been made about nine years previously hadn't deterred the powers-that-be; nor for that matter had the incident when he appeared on stage drunk during his last visit. Therefore, full of hope and still in search of international stardom, he signed the contract.

I tried my best to talk him out of it. The thought of his being alone in a strange country for three months with no one to care for him or understand him filled me with dread. But he was firm, determined, and once Tony made his mind up about something nothing could move him. So, wrapped in fear, I went along with his plans.

Meanwhile, he told me, he was going to dry out completely, this time for good. I promised him that if he stayed dry for a year, I would leave John again and marry him. The actress had faded away and Lily came to stay with him. All seemed well until the phone rang early one morning (mercifully John had an early start on a film). It was Lily begging me to come over immediately as Tony was ill. I arrived to find him in a coma. In the small hours of the morning he had walked into her room, announced that he had drunk a bottle of brandy in five minutes and passed out. His usual doctor was away and Lily had found a local doctor, a stranger, who was unfamiliar with Tony and his problems and at a loss to know what to do. Tony was lying on the bed; his face was bloated, his eyelids and lips were swollen and his skin had a bluish tinge. Lily and the doctor were attempting to rouse him.

Unfortunately the doctor was a Scot, and Tony, for some obscure reason, hated the Scottish accent. On hearing the doctor speak, Tony's first coherent words were 'fuck off'. The goodly doctor ignored this invitation and asked him if he wanted to die? A heartfelt 'Yes!' came from between the blue and swollen lips – a need to be fulfilled all too soon.

So, helped by massive injections of vitamins, Tony pulled through that day. By the evening he was again vowing to dry out and prepare for the future. From that time on I personally never saw him drink again. I think that last crisis had been an attempt at cure by revulsion. If he survived, then he would go on with the battle; if he failed, so be it. Russian roulette.

Having survived, once more he had a future on which to hook his hopes: he set about preparing to conquer Australia. The following months were too intimate to write about in detail and I guard them jealously because I spent them with the real Tony. He was strong, sexy, considerate towards me and very determined. No fears were voiced and no doubts, there was only the possibility of his success to hang on to now because failure was too terrible to contemplate. It was his last chance and he had to take it alone. The feeling between us was deeper than passion and softened by melancholy. I was to know the same feeling again later in my life . . . first when John was dying, and later with my father. It was a time when I had to give my best with respect and without drama because there was nothing else to be done. There was no escape from the reality of what was happening; each moment required a higher awareness and understanding so that every word and gesture could be filed away in a special place for a rainy day.

Our last weekend arrived and naturally I spent it with him, as I had spent every available moment during the past few months. I am not proud of deceiving my husband, but that's what I did, every available moment that God gave me. And thankfully, in so doing I accumulated for myself some memories to set as salvage against Tony's loss.

On our last night together we couldn't make love – we

didn't try. We were casual, almost offhand with each other. I packed his case in readiness for the morning and after he had taken his sleeping pills we went to bed for a final clamp. He fell asleep with his head on my shoulder and one leg across me. It was the most uncomfortable night I've ever spent, but I was afraid to move and lose one inch of his closeness.

We hardly spoke the next morning, we didn't dare in case we became too emotional. We left the flat together with our bags packed, I bound for Ramsgate and he for Heathrow. He kept the taxi waiting at Victoria so that he could take me to the platform, but halfway across the concourse he suddenly said, 'I'm leaving you here,' gave me a long hard look, kissed me firmly and left. Cheated of my last few seconds with him, but understanding even his small self-denial of the theatrical gesture of waving me goodbye, I went home to Ramsgate and got on with my life.

An odd coincidence, a sort of karmic retribution, happened. While shopping in Kensington High Street one day, I was stopped by a man I had met many years before when we had both been employed by a so-called private detective agency which specialized in obtaining evidence for divorces. At that time I had just met John, and I was still looking for ways to supplement my income. I had met the man at a party and he had suggested that I should join the agency, and within a few weeks he had fixed me up with a job which involved a Russian artist who frequented a club in Earls Court.

I was hired to watch the man in order to find out if he was sleeping with anyone, and if so to report back to the agency who would then put him under surveillance. The artist's wife had left him, wanted to marry a title, and to pin the blame on the poor fellow without a breath of scandal touching her noble intended. While this didn't appeal to my left-wing tendencies at all, I needed the capitalist money, so I was given membership of the club, and armed with a photograph of the poor artist and, taking a girl friend along for appearance's sake, off I went to find out what he was up to.

I hadn't been in the club more than half an hour when the very fellow I was trailing made himself known to me and asked us to join a large table full of friendly Russians who were celebrating a birthday. They were all fairly drunk but amiable enough, especially my victim, who was also maudlin, and who by the end of the evening, without any prompting from me, had told me the sad tale of the wife who had left him for another and broken his heart.

So touched was I by all this Russian melancholy, let alone by the copious amounts of vodka placed before me, that at the end of the evening I took him home and gave him what can only be described as a good seeing-to. After a few days I reported back to the agency that the man was above reproach and devoted to his wife.

After that I did the more straightforward job of being a private co-respondent which involved spending a night or two in a hotel room with a man seeking a divorce. There was never the slightest degree of danger involved as all the clients used this odd procedure in order to protect the honour of someone they wished to marry, and they were, without exception, respectable members of society, some famous, some titled. I enjoyed the work which, apart from being well paid, involved being taken out for a sumptuous dinner before going back to the hotel room, quite often to play Scrabble. In the morning the waiter would bring breakfast to the room, report that he had seen us sitting in our twin beds, and that was all there was to it.

Due to the incongruous situation, all my clients were much more nervous than I, so sometimes I arranged to meet up and introduce them to John during the course of the evening which set their minds at rest that all was above board, and on several occasions I was asked to meet the lady involved in order to prove that I wasn't a call girl out to seduce her intended.

I made many friends this way and heard many stories, all of them highly confidential. Therefore it was ironic that the same agency I had worked for in so many divorces was now on my tail, and even more amazing that it never once occurred to me on meeting the fellow in the street that I was now the prey.

I had arranged a box number in Ramsgate for Tony to write to. Looking back at his letters now, the box number seems a reproach – even our letters had to be exchanged in secret. He began to write during the stop-off in India, where he stayed with his friend John Freeman and his wife to break the journey. He said everyone looked and sounded like blacked-up Peter Sellers' with Welsh accents. The next letter came from Australia, written the day he arrived there. As soon as I had his address I wrote to him every day; it was almost like keeping a diary. Writing kept us sane and the parting a little more bearable. The post was erratic, however; there were days when I received nothing, then several letters would arrive together.

His letters were almost shy, with no passion or eroticism in them – he had a fear of sounding sentimental – but they were full of love all the same. More than anything, they conveyed his true feelings. Mercifully they are the one tangible thing of his that remain.

I carried them everywhere, rereading them incessantly, analysing them with microscopic obsessiveness and guarding them jealously. No one read them. Eighteen years after Tony's death I showed them to my son David, and he burst into tears on reading them. Each one ended with the entreaty to me not to let our love fade, to hold on to what we had and be strong. He would describe this or that experience, a script conference, a show, or a cricket match in which he met the players and they gazed at each other in mutual awe, and say that they helped to dull the pain of our separation. Many times he wrote that the temptation to go to the airport and come home to me was overwhelming. 'If only Australia could be moved a little closer to Ramsgate,' one letter said.

If he could have got straight to work, all would have been well, but there were delays. A director couldn't be found until Eddie Joffe, a South African working for Grampian TV, was persuaded to take the job, but he couldn't go to Australia immediately, which was fatal. Tony began to drink and his letters ceased. Lily rang me – she became the intermediary when he wanted to speak to me.

Sometimes I would call from home, reversing the charges, sometimes from his flat. Each time he denied that he was drinking but begged me to go out to him – if only I'd had the courage. Then he moved to Sydney, where there was a showdown, a crisis, and he was told to dry out or else! He went on a cure and the letters began again, leaving in their wake a telephone bill that cost him over £1000. He embarked on another economy drive. 'If you need to speak to me,' he said, 'ring direct and I'll reimburse you later.' I had to laugh – once more he had swung from extravagance to frugality, but I didn't dare phone him from home as the telephone bill would have given the game away. Yet again he was full of hope. 'I'm going to beat the hell out of them and then beat the hell out of Australia,' he wrote.

His divorce from Freddie was imminent. He was afraid of the bad publicity that her revelations would invite and was worried that she might claim alimony from him. He was also terrified that I would be cited, as of course I was. One day two reporters called at my home. Instead of slamming the door on them I tried to bluff my way out by saying that the affair between Tony and me was over. The *Sunday Express* printed the story of the divorce on the front page. At the same time there was a postal strike in Australia and my letters to him were delayed. The newspaper article and the lack of letters convinced Tony that I had abandoned him. In his state of insecurity it was all he needed.

The very last time I heard from Tony I received two letters on the same day: one, sent to my box number, was the most loving and tender that he had ever written. 'My Love, My Love, My Love,' he wrote, 'What else is there to say but this? All will be well, just hold on to the fact that we will be together in time.' The other was enclosed inside a letter to my mother in which he apologized for all the pain he had caused my parents and said that he would have no further contact with me. To me he wrote: 'I loved you more than I thought possible, but now I realize that you never shared this feeling. I now relinquish you to your own life and will forget you in time. You admonished me many times about wasting my life. Now I say the same to you. I shall not brood over you. In a few weeks our relationship will be dead, cold and unremembered.'

I don't know why I didn't go straight to the phone and ring him then and there. But I decided to wait until the next day and ring him from London – there was always someone around in Ramsgate.

Then John rang from Rome saying that he would be home the next day and that evening I rushed back to London to call Tony during the night, but he was in rehearsal. Then John arrived, full of news, taking my attention . . .

On John's first night home we decided to go out to dinner. While I was getting ready I heard on the radio an orchestral version of 'Here's That Rainy Day' and a strong feeling of Tony came over me. It was so overwhelming that I wanted to ring him immediately, but John was there, so once more the opportunity was lost.

That night we went out with friends to a restaurant in Covent Garden and afterwards to a jazz club, arriving home in the small hours. Early the next morning the phone rang while I was in the middle of a deep sleep. John answered it. It rang again immediately after he'd hung up, and then rang yet again. 'Who the hell keeps ringing this early?' I asked, half asleep. I turned over. John was sitting on the side of the bed.

'Are you properly awake?' he asked.

'Of course I am, with all the phone calls,' I answered.

'Then sit up, I have something to tell you. It was on the news this morning from Australia . . .'

I didn't want to hear any more. I put my hands over my ears. 'Don't tell me. Don't say it,' I kept repeating.

Tony had taken pills, lots of them, barbiturates, washed down with vodka. Until then he had been dry. His decision had been made cold-bloodedly and in sobriety during the terrible depression that always followed a dry-out.

He had left a note: 'Too many things seemed to go wrong,' he'd written. There was nothing for me – I had already received mine.

Two months later my mother told me that Lily had phoned her on the day before he died, saying that Tony wanted to speak to me to make up. 'She will come back to me, won't she?' he'd asked her. 'Of course she will,' Lily'd said, and she'd tried to track me down. When she phoned London, I was out shopping, so she rang Ramsgate, to be told by my mother that I was in Rome with John, that it was best to leave things as they were.

It was fortunate that I didn't learn of this until later. I was demented with grief at the time, and would probably have turned on my mother if I'd known. In my anguish she would have become the butt of all my sorrow. As it was she suffered quite enough while having to carry that secret about with her. She still does suffer, I know, but at the time she had seen only the pain we were causing John and thought she was doing the right thing by trying to protect him.

When the fact that Tony was dead finally hit me I remember raging at him. 'You stupid bastard.' I screamed. 'You rotten coward!' If his spirit was close by me, it must have winced at my wrath.

Then I turned on John, who didn't know what to do with me. He had never seen anger like this before. I blamed him for being alive, for winning. It all came out: the truth of what I'd felt for Tony, the fact that I'd carried on seeing him behind John's back, that I had planned to leave John and marry Tony. 'If I'd gone with him he'd be alive now,' I yelled, completely out of control. My behaviour was terrible, but I couldn't stop. John called Tony's doctor, who came over and sedated me, and when the injection began to take its merciful effect, the tears came, and with them the realization that I would never see him again.

There was nothing in the world that I could do to bring him back, no way to tell him how very much I loved him, how sorry I was for not telling him more often, for not being strong enough. Then the drug took over and I slept.

David rang in the evening. He had heard the news early that morning. He told me later that the fact that I was probably still sleeping and didn't know was the worst thing of all. He had gone upstairs and cried his heart out when my parents, in a lame attempt at consolation said, 'It's all for the best'.

Lily rang. 'Isn't it awful?' she said. 'Are you all right?'

But I was too deep in shock to comfort her. I could only nod at the phone. It was my first loss, my first bereavement, and I couldn't handle it.

That week, the worst in my life, was paced out by the blessed oblivion of sleep – the nightmares of waking. John wandered about like a ghost himself. Hattie, who understood my feelings completely, phoned and implored me (too late I fear) not to take it out on him because he was alive and Tony wasn't.

Sometimes I woke from the sedatives to find someone babysitting me so that John could go out, away from me and my pervasive sorrow. Once Mark, my first husband, came and sat with me. Like John, he didn't know what to do either. 'I've never lost anyone and I don't know how it feels,' he said.

'It feels wonderful,' I said, drunk on tranquillizers, hardly able to see him through eyelids water-blistered from weeping. I must have borne a striking resemblance to Edward G. Robinson.

One morning Lynn, our daily, brought me a cup of tea. 'Come on now,' she said. 'He had reached copper bottom after all.' At the thought of how much Tony would have loved the remark I burst out laughing, spilling tea all over her.

Johnny Hendricks, the jazz singer, came over to see me one evening. I was still in bed, too weak, too depressed to get up, except to drag myself to the bathroom. I wanted only the escape of sleep.

'If you really loved the guy,' he said, 'you'd respect his memory. Don't lie there full of self-pity. He'd had enough of his life. Now be a fighter like he was and get on with yours, because it's still going on out there.'

He was right, of course: somewhere beyond the pain, in the future, life was beckoning me back. It still had some gifts to bring me along with a number of left hooks and rainy days.

Fourteen

The memorial service for Tony was imminent, the press were hanging around the flat, and John didn't know what to do with me. As for me, I didn't care about anything. Waking up was like a horror movie, finding myself in a wet, sodden nightmare; only sleep was full of peace and sweet dreams.

But of course I couldn't go on like that. John was almost at the end of his tether – he never was any good at looking after people and my grief was too much for anyone. Eventually he took matters into his own hands and sent me away. My cousin Marion was in Marbella, so he sent her a telegram saying that I was coming, booked me a first-class ticket, and implored me to get out of bed and fuck off. So I shakily got to my feet the night before my departure in order to rehearse walking.

John saw me off at the airport. Sandy Fawkes, a longstanding journalist friend of mine, came too to give him some female support. After a few large vodkas they pushed me into the departure lounge, where I wandered around for a while, clutching a pile of books they had bought for me, and somehow managed to miss the flight. As I staggered out of the departure lounge in floods of tears, I found them at the bar. Holding on to the last remnants of his endurance, John managed to book me on another flight to Malaga. What an incredible sense of relief he must have felt to see me go, and how fortunate for me that he still wanted me back when I'd sorted myself out.

Marion and Dinny were waiting at Malaga airport. They had been there all day and during the long wait

Marion found an old newspaper which contained news of Tony's death. John hadn't mentioned it in the telegram, assuming that, as it was world news, they would have realized why I was going out to join them.

I arrived at midnight, white, wasted and slightly demented. Dinny had just finished the stunt driving for a film called *The Great Race* and he was hyped up from weeks of rushing around hairpin bends on precarious mountain passes. Nevertheless, as was his nature, he was kind and patient. He understood, in a no-nonsense, masculine sort of way, how deeply shocked I was by Tony's suicide – it was such a deep rejection of all that I had thought existed between us. His remedy was the 'If you're looking for sympathy it's in the dictionary between "shit" and "suicide" ' approach, and he tried to keep me busy, with lots of exercise and *divertissements*. He found me a gigolo, a handsome beach bum named Benito. Due to his lack of Spanish Dinny had formed the impression that Benito was an interior decorator, but it turned out that the cafés and restaurants that Benny proudly pointed out to us with a flourish had been painted, not designed, by him.

Benito must have seen me as the answer to a gigolo's prayer. He thought I was the widow of a famous man, due to my habit of bursting into tears in the most embarrassing places for no apparent reason. So, from day one, he launched into a full-scale campaign to insinuate himself into my heart, knickers and bank account, in that order.

Poor Benny must have invested quite a bit of his capital in the project, because the first few outings were on him. He was always supporting me, literally holding me up at times when I had knocked back a few too many, which I was doing with increasing regularity under the mistaken belief that one really could drown one's sorrows. '*Mi pequeña enferma*,' Benny would say, as he held my hand in some late-night bar or other. '*Mi corazón*,' his beautiful Spanish eyes spilling over with tears of simulated sympathy. '*Yo medico*,' he would declare, striking his chest in a Tarzanesque manner. Poor Benito, he was really a very simple fellow.

Marbella in those days still had some character. It was a small town with outlying houses, instead of what it is now – part of an ugly chain of skyscraper hotels and apartment blocks on either side of a busy motorway. The main road was still pot-holed and picturesque with grassy verges. Our hotel was situated a short lurch out of the village. It was rustic and quite small, and comprised a semicircle of rooms, grouped around a swimming pool and each with its own little forecourt. There was a dining room and a bar, but its chief assets were the lawns and the flowerbeds with the swimming pool in the centre.

To the side of the hotel was a pine-tree-shaded dirt track which led down to the beach on which was a bamboo-covered bar where, in between his painting jobs, the prowling Benito would search for rich widows.

Dinny would leave us girls cavorting in the shallows and take off sometimes to the far horizon, where he would explore the deeps, the tip of his orange snorkel appearing above the water from time to time, spouting like a basking whale, and then disappearing with a flick of a black rubber flipper. He would bring us gifts from the sea bed, large lovely shells, and once a revolting black sea slug which resembled a perambulating penis, and which Marion made him take back whence it came.

Dear Dinny, sadly his and Marion's eight-year-old relationship was drawing to an end. Marion, who throughout the eight years that they had been together had never looked to anyone else for either sex or companionship, was beginning to get restless. She was relieved when Dinny cut short his holiday after I had been there about a week as he had the chance of another stunt job. Marion was only too happy to stay on to keep an eye on me and it was great to have her there.

On the very first night of Dinny's departure, Benito, who had pledged to look after us, showed himself in his true colours. He was holding my hand in a late-night bar

and went into one of his '*Tu enferma, Yo medico*' routines.
He then proceeded to explain how he was in love with me
and how lovely it would be if the two of us could go away
to a little village in the mountains where we could make
love all day and where I could forget my sadness. The
trouble was, he wistfully added, it would cost money, as
he had many responsibilities and he had to work hard to
make ends meet, thereby exploding the myth about the
successful interior decorator and the jolly reliable fellow, in
one fell swoop.

Fate, or Tony's spirit, was definitely on my side during
that time, as not long afterwards his irate and much malig-
ned wife turned up with their two children and caught him
'entertaining' a French woman who had to make an undig-
nified retreat through the bedroom window of his cottage,
while his wife belaboured poor Benito about the head with
her handbag.

As it was, it didn't take me long to start tarting about.
What the hell, I reassured, I had to get through the rest of
my life without Tony and I didn't intend to miss out on
anything that would help to make a diversion from the
pain and emptiness that I was feeling. It was always worse
at night, so an amorous companion was almost a must
during that crazy time.

The first one was an English actor, an oily charmer with
a drink problem. I poured out my sad story to him and
took him to bed to take my mind off things for the odd
hour or so, but he didn't last more than a few days. He
tried to cheer me up one evening in a bar by doing Hancock impersonations, much to Marion's disgust. 'How
tasteless,' she said subtly, and that was that. Poor bugger,
it wasn't his fault – it was just that nobody could erase my
anguish or replace the love I had lost. Nobody ever did.
Only John came close, but in a different way.

From then I lurched from one sordid affair to another,
drifting through under an umbrella of antidepressants and
tranquillizers which I took in vast quantities.

We ran out of money – in those days the English cheque

wasn't as acceptable as it is now. The only thing to do was go to Gibraltar, so off we went in a bumpy coach over what was then a dirt road to Algeciras where we boarded the ferry for the Rock. At the bank in Gibraltar we were informed that my cheque would take twenty-four hours to clear, so we decided to make a two-day stop-over and see the sights, naïvely thinking that Gibraltar would be bursting with life and gaiety.

That evening we set off by taxi to a night club, which had been recommended by the waiters at the hotel. It turned out to be a big disappointment. We inquired on entering if there was a cabaret, and were told that we were early – the club didn't fill up until at least twelve o'clock. Then we were led into a small, sleazy room with a bar at the back along which lounged a few lizards, who stared at us indolently through a haze of cigarette smoke. There was a tiny stage and a few tables arranged around the room. We looked about us with growing apprehension. 'I don't like the look of this,' said Marion nervously. 'We're the only women in the place.'

A waiter came over for our order. 'What is the cabaret tonight?' I asked.

'Oh, very good, you will enjoy,' he answered. 'We have striptease girls who take off their clothes, and then the men come on stage and the girls take off men's clothes and everybody laugh.'

We reached silently for our handbags. 'We will come back later,' I said, giving a brave attempt at a smile, and we beat a hasty retreat.

The friendly taxi driver was still outside the dive when we shot out of the door. We hailed him like a long-lost friend, leaped into the back of the taxi and told him to take us to the safety of the Rock Hotel.

The taxi driver, whose name was Frank, told us that he was a guide and arranged tours of the Rock during the day. If we liked he would give us the de-luxe tour the next day at a very special price. 'Why not?' I said. 'By the look of things I will probably never come back here again if I can possibly help it. So let's see what it has to offer in the daylight.'

We arranged that Frank should pick us up at a little restaurant by the harbour the next morning. He turned out by the light of day to be much younger than we had first thought. He took us first to see the caves, which were very impressive, with their giant stalactites and stalagmites forming weird and wonderful shapes, like a cathedral with great stone organ pipes. It was at moments like this that, while I was looking at something I had never seen before in a place I had never before been, Tony faded away and left me in peace for an hour or so. Then suddenly the smallest thing, and he and the pain would rush back and start hammering at me again, and all the colour and joy would leave the world.

After our tour, which included a visit to the baboons, Frank suggested that he and a friend of his should take us out that evening and show us Gibraltar. Rather than be left alone in the hotel, where the ghost of Tony would be sure to grab me, I accepted his invitation, albeit with grave foreboding.

There was nothing wrong with my date that a young and innocent Spanish girl of twenty would have found fault with. Pedro was a perfectly nice, simple young man of about twenty-two, swarthy, broad-shouldered, with long sideburns and a comb that was produced with monotonous regularity throughout the evening. He spoke very little English, which didn't help the conversation, but what was worse, he fancied me. Marion and Frank were getting on like a house on fire, however, and showed no signs of wanting to part. All I could do was grin and bear it, and drink.

We ended up in a caravan down by the harbour. Apparently it was owned jointly by a number of local lads who used it as a place to take their girlfriends. So there we were, sitting in this sordid little knocking shop on wheels and swigging whisky from a bottle as it passed from hand to hand. We had to leave when one of the part owners turned up with his girlfriend, and so we staggered to the beach. By this time the horizon was tilting dangerously. Marion and Frank disappeared and I found myself spread-eagled underneath my young friend who, before I realized what was happening, fucked me with the speed of a pouter pigeon, just giving himself time to roll clear before I vomited up the entire evening's amnesia recipe.

Somehow I made my way back to my hotel room and from there I greeted the grinning dawn with the realization that carrying on in this fashion would not do. The booze was only increasing the depressions and getting me into some very dicey situations. The previous night's episode was deeply shaming; it had also frightened me. I resolved to try harder, to get better for John's sake. Some of what I was doing was a way of revenging myself against Tony. Underneath my sorrow I was angry. If he was haunting me, as I believed, deep down, he really was, I wanted to do something that would make him suffer for rejecting so finally and so spitefully all that there had been between us.

I wanted to get back to Spain and away from Gibraltar as soon as possible. Marion decided to stay a few more days, having fallen breathlessly in love with Frank. 'What shall I say if Dinny calls?' I asked ungraciously, not wanting to be on my own.

'Oh, darling, you'll think of something,' said my lovesick cousin, so off I went back to Marbella, hung over, depressed, and having lost a large slice of my self-esteem.

When I finally arrived at the hotel after a sour and dusty ride on the primitive motorcoach I knew something was wrong the moment I entered the foyer. There was a pall of silence over the place, a muted feeling of oppression. As I walked to my room through the garden I saw that the swimming pool had been drained. There was only a hand-ful of guests sitting outside their rooms. One of them, a young French girl called Sofie, came over and explained what had happened.

There had been an English couple staying at the hotel. They had been there for about a week and we had struck a friendship with them before we went to Gibraltar. They were in their mid-sixties, and the husband was a retired army officer. They were both on their second marriage, having spent years extricating themselves from their first ones. They had only been married two years and were quite obviously in love. They were in the habit of joining us for a drink in the evenings with Sofie and some of the other young guests, and, as one does, we had all opened up about our private lives far more than we would have done at home.

They were a couple of thoroughly nice people, so it was a particularly nasty shock to learn of the death that very morning of the husband. At about seven o'clock he had gone for his usual walk before breakfast and when he didn't return his wife had gone to look for him. She asked the young boy at the reception desk if he had seen him, and the boy had gone into the garden with her to see if they could find him. It was while they were standing by the pool that he looked down and saw the husband lying under the water. With great presence of mind the young lad whisked her away before she had seen the body in the pretence of taking her to look for her husband on the beach.

As he passed the reception desk the boy told the other clerk in rapid Spanish what had happened, and took her out of the hotel while the staff got the man out. Edith, the wife, told me later that during the walk she looked at the boy and saw that his eyes were full of tears and she knew then that her husband was dead. It seemed that he had never learned to swim and must have tripped over a piece of crazy paving at the edge of the pool, fallen into the deep end and panicked.

To me it all seemed so much worse because they were so happy and had been dragged apart by such a small mischance, unlike my situation in which at least Tony had made the choice to leave. And suddenly there was the anger again. I can remember mentally berating him about that tragic incident many times during the week I spent with Edith while she was waiting for clearance to take her husband's body home. 'Do you see what it's like?' I told him. 'Well, you *chose* to inflict the same kind of pain on to me.'

I was always having long conversations with Tony, and I swear that he answered me. I could hear his voice in my head as clearly as anyone else's. I was sure that his unhappy soul was earthbound, and for my part I wanted to make it more unhappy for leaving me.

As for poor Edith, who could understand her pain better than I? And so I stayed close to her, having meals with her, walking with her, and staying up until the small hours while she relived her years with her husband, weighing and balancing every sentence that had passed between them, finding portents and double meanings in every moment of their recent past to preserve in her memory for the lonely years that were inevitably waiting.

On her last evening we had dinner together, helped down by a large quantity of wine. I told her how impressed I was by her courage during that awful week. She said that from then on she resolved to live in a way that would make her husband proud of her, otherwise everything that they had shared and all that they had learned from each other would mean nothing and might as well have never happened. In the light of her quiet acceptance and dignity, I began to feel vastly ashamed of my noisy grief. There was absolutely nothing in my recent behaviour to make Tony proud to have known me, what with my anger, screwing around and boozing. The example of Edith was a salutary lesson to me.

The million-to-one chance that took me to that particular hotel at the same time as Edith in order to meet someone suffering as I was leads me to believe, as I look down through the past years at the apparently unrelated jumble of happenings, that there is a jigsaw of coincidences which fit into place in the scheme of things, and that everything, however bad, is ultimately for our growth. Edith left to bury her dead, the swimming pool was filled, more guests came and went, and we stayed on, and on, and on . . .

John phoned me three or four times a week. He never asked me when I was coming home, just inquired how I was, but I knew it was time to begin to think about going back to England. My conscience was beginning to prick, which I suppose was a healthy sign, but the truth was that I didn't feel ready to take any responsibility as yet, I didn't want anybody to lean on me until I was stronger. John also had been abused and hurt, and I had a lot of work ahead repairing the damage I had done to him over the past two years. But I didn't want to go home still in bits and pieces, so I waited.

All this while Marion was having the time of her life. She had hurled her bonnet over the windmill and gone for broke. She knew her relationship with Dinny was at an end. He had also phoned several times but, unlike John, he had ordered her to return home. She had flatly refused. She had found herself a job as an extra on a movie which was being made out there, cavorting round a swimming pool as a flower child. She had a herd of young admirers, the director of the movie was after her, and she was being wined, dined, flattered and bonked.

Then one weekend, much to my acute embarrassment, Frank, the Gibraltarian taxi driver, came to Marbella, bringing with him his friend Pedro, the gay seducer. Marion begged me to make up a foursome, which was about the last thing I wanted to do. In the end I agreed to have dinner with them at a restaurant in the village, on condition that I could come back early pleading a headache. Over dinner Pedro, who had cottoned on to the fact that I had no intention of repeating the mistakes of our previous meeting, was growing morose, drinking heavily and giving me reproachful looks, backed up by Marion, who wore a 'Can't you even be nice to him?' expression. I was getting very angry.

I stood up, suddenly determined. 'I have got a terrible headache and I'm going to bed.' I ignored the hurt looks on everyone's face and fled. I had suddenly become bored with the whole silly business. What the hell was I doing? None of it mattered to me one jot or tittle, only Tony mattered and he was gone for ever . . . The tears began, the flood of hopelessness that washed away nothing and left me weak and swollen brimmed up and spilled over.

I didn't want to see anyone or go anywhere, I just wanted to be alone. I was passing a quiet little bar, so I mopped myself up as best I could and went inside, ordered a brandy and water, and found a quiet table where I sat with my back to the room gulping and moping until I was under control. I made the decision to go home. I didn't feel strong enough and I wasn't sure if I could hide these dreadful avalanches of grief or how long it would take before the pain subsided, but I wasn't doing a very good job out here either. It was time to leave. I would book my ticket tomorrow.

Having made up my mind, I felt better. I looked around. There was a man sitting at the bar whom I recognized. I had seen him on the beach on several occasions with an adorable little girl of about three, his daughter I assumed. He seemed interesting, and rather mysterious. He came over. 'What are you doing here?' he said. 'I've never seen you in this bar before.'

'I just wanted to be on my own for a while and have a think, and this was the first place at hand,' I answered. 'But I'm fine now,' I added hastily. 'Don't go away.'

He didn't. In fact, he stayed with me for the rest of the night, or rather I stayed with him. He had rented a beautiful villa just outside the village, having recently absconded from England with his daughter. His marriage had foundered, his wife had fallen in love with someone else, and he couldn't face life without seeing his daughter again, so he had uprooted himself from everything and was virtually on the run. I felt sorry for him – for all his money, his life was full of conflict and loneliness. He probably had a ruthless streak and could be a hard man to live with, but for me at that moment he was fine. We told each other our life stories and offered each other mutual consolation. I gave him my company and he gave me somewhere to hide away from the pettifogging problems that I had created. It was a fair exchange. I shall call him Charles.

He drove me back to the hotel after a day spent playing around his swimming pool with his daughter and preparing a poolside lunch for the four of us, his housekeeper included. It was fun, and more normal than anything that had happened to me recently – I particularly enjoyed pottering about in the kitchen. It all served to intensify my decision to go home. I had been away from England and my family for six weeks. We were at the end of August, autumn was waiting.

So was Marion when I reached the hotel, waiting and worried. After all, she was supposed to be there to keep an eye on me and I was a bit potty. The boys had departed for Gibraltar after a rather drunken night during which she had trailed them round the clubs and discos looking for someone to take poor Pedro off her hands. I told her of my decision to go home. I wanted her to come too, but she was reluctant to leave. She was having a good time in Marbella and dreading the showdown with Dinny when she finally returned to England.

So I went to the travel agents and booked a one-way ticket home. Three days later Charles picked me up at the hotel and took me to the airport. On the plane I was befriended by a British Airways pilot returning from holiday. He sat next to me and held my hand during take-off and landing and delivered me safely into the care of my dear, patient, long-suffering John.

The flat depressed me more than words can say. It was like going back into another world. The bedroom, where Tony and I had spent our first night together, where I had heard the news of his death and experienced the fresh new pain of bereavement, felt as though my sorrow pervaded its walls like mist. Deep down in my guts was the knowledge that there was nothing to be done but endure and a panicky fear that I might not be able to. Above all I knew that I had to be nice and kind to John, when all I wanted to do was cry like a child and say, 'I love someone else so much that I don't want to go on living without him.' How could I say that to a good, sensitive man like John? Even with the kindest person in the world there are certain truths that cannot be shared.

We went out to dinner that night. As we drove to the restaurant I realized that along every street in London there would be a memory waiting. Every day I would have to pass the flat where Tony and I had lived together and the little restaurant opposite, where we had eaten so many times, said so many things to each other, and from where he had dragged me in a fit of lust the night I showed him my garter. The theatres we had visited, and the cinemas, the parks, the zoo, the shops, the pubs – they were all still there like empty shells of memories, and he was gone, irrevocably lost to me for ever. I could wail like a banshee, beat my head against the wall, beg him to haunt me for ever, but nothing would ever give me one minute more of him, not one more look or one more touch. He was gone . . .

In the restaurant I listened to John telling me what had happened in my absence, trying to react and smile in the right places, dodging questions about Spain that might have had a man in the answer, telling him what he wanted to hear. 'Yes, I had a lovely rest. Yes, I feel much better. Yes, I was homesick.' He never asked me if I loved him; I don't think he ever asked that question. For John that would have been very presumptuous. But over dinner I did tell him I loved him, and of course it was true, but not in the way I loved Tony. Never again would I love anyone like that. That love belonged to Tony, and he had taken it with him.

The spring of 1968 had brought a godsend into our lives, although we didn't know it at the time. It was *Dad's Army*, a little package of six scripts about life in the Home Guard during the war. Neither of us thought it was anything out of the ordinary, just the average bread-and-butter job that would survive six episodes. Instead it brought us a new way of life, a little more security over the next ten years, and some very loving friends. By the time I returned from Spain wearing my crown of thorns, John was digging into the part and the public were beginning to take notice. As a lot of the filming was done in Thetford, Norfolk, John was away for long periods of time. Sometimes the wives of the cast would go to the locations for the odd visit, but normally the men preferred to be alone together. It was like a rather exclusive club: everyone got on well together, genuinely admired each other's talent, and they all made each other laugh a lot.

John was full of it. Over dinner on my first night he spoke of nothing else. His eyes were soft with an inner contentment and he talked about the cast and the work. After all that he had put up with over the previous two years nobody deserved it more. On top of that he had me back. Heaven knows why he wanted me, but he did. So, bruised and battered though I was, and missing a few parts, I crept back into my home and the shelter of my husband's love.

Fifteen

In the year following Tony's death I went through the classic pattern of bereavement. I compared everything with what had happened the previous year. Barely an hour passed when I was free from thinking about him. I would wake up in the morning having forgotten him. Then, with the first stirring of memory, the pain would start deep down, like the beginning of a labour spasm in childbirth. As reality encroached I would feel the anguish slowly coming towards me like a tidal wave.

The worst part was the feeling of impotence: there was no way to reach him, no way back, no chance of a single, precious minute in which to make my farewell. It put me in such a turmoil that I would break into a sweat and, if John was there, I would have to rush to the bathroom to be alone until I had calmed down.

John knew the bottom of my grief, although he never commented on it. If we were in bed and I began to struggle to hold back the tears, he would feign sleep or sometimes give me a pat on the shoulder, nothing more, for he knew I would suffocate if he gave me sympathy.

One day in Ramsgate I came across a Victorian terraced house for sale. It was going cheap, clean as a whistle, furnished with some heavy yet practical pieces, garishly wallpapered, but with great potential and good vibrations. John didn't even want to look at it before we signed the contract – he was happy to trust my judgement. So the sale was made and we owned our first home. In a fever of homemaking I embarked on redecorating, burning up a lot of energy and anguish painting walls rather than banging my head against them. It turned out to be good therapy.

John was content for me to be in Ramsgate doing something constructive at last. The first time he saw the house his armchair was in front of the fire and it was functioning as a home.

Working on the house gave me the excuse I needed to sleep alone, because the night-time was when I wrote to Tony. It may sound dotty, but it was the best way I could find to get close to him. I would look forward to bedtime because the hours before sleep were for him. It was then that I reread his precious letters and wrote to him as though he were still alive.

It was during this period that three strange things happened. First, the watch that Tony had bought for me in Hong Kong mysteriously stopped. When I worked out the time difference between England and Australia, it had stopped at exactly the time he died. I continued to wear it, but left it set as it was and didn't wind it, as I took it to be a message from him.

The next strange event concerned our cleaner who looked after the new house. She was a sensible soul, so it was rather a shock when she suddenly told me that she had seen Tony Hancock sitting in the living room 'as large as life'. Her description of his posture and how he was dressed was so accurate there was no way that she could have imagined it. It is possible that she had heard the odd rumour about our relationship, but I certainly hadn't told her anything about us. Anyway, according to her he was smiling, so I like to think that the apparition was genuine. Although I couldn't understand why he hadn't shown himself to me, nevertheless it was comforting to feel that he was so close, and that helped me through the first year.

The third strange happening occurred just after the first anniversary of Tony's death. John, David and I went to a show at the Pavilion Theatre, Ramsgate, the theatre where I had worked in the box office all those years ago. As I sat in the stalls between John and David I suddenly felt a rush of happiness. It was so strong it made me shudder. I looked from one to the other of them – they were both laughing at something on the stage – and I felt such a wave of love for them that I suddenly knew that everything was going to be all right. When I looked at my watch it had started again. I may have wound it myself without realizing, but I believe that it was another rush of energy from some unknown source that had set the hands in motion. Whatever the cause, from that moment I began to get better.

As the years passed the hurt faded. The most positive thing that came out of it all was my love for John and the gift of as good a marriage as anyone could hope for. The twenty years we spent together were the best years of my life, even though I didn't know it at the time. I was never in love with John – I distrust that emotion intensely because it can vanish as swiftly as it appears, and what I felt for John, though it lacked passion, is indestructible.

John said that it taught him never to take anyone or anything for granted. But then, I never thought he did. For my part, it took me a good many years to stop taking him for granted. I carried a lot of anger for far too long. But not against John, against life.

John was due to go to Marrakesh to work on a film and I decided to go with him. Six weeks in the sun, no memories, and lots of new people to meet. I fell in love with one of them, but John didn't mind. His name was Wilfrid Hyde White, one of the most amusing men I have ever met. He and John were two of a kind, and as Wilfrid was alone John and I had dinner with him almost every night. Between the two of them no one could have asked for better company.

Wilfrid was full of idiosyncracies. He was always cold. Even in the heat of Morocco he always wore a waistcoat, overcoat and scarf. Wrapped up in this fashion, he would sit by the hotel pool enjoying a drink with John, while I swam, accompanied by his entreaties not to catch my death of cold in ninety degrees Fahrenheit.

Terry Thomas was also appearing in the film and he asked me if I would dress up as a Moroccan woman in black robes and yashmak and pose with him for some publicity photographs. After the session and still wearing the robes, I went over to John and Wilfrid, who were having their customary lunchtime drinks by the pool. I didn't say anything – I simply stared at them.

'What's the matter, dear?' asked Wilfrid.

I continued to stare in silence.

'You try, Johnny. See what she wants,' said Wilfrid.

'Perhaps she wants money,' John suggested, and he held some out to me.

I jumped back as if horrified.

'Oh dear, I hate to be rude to these people, but I wish I knew the Moroccan for "Fuck off",' said Wilfrid.

Thereupon I blew a raspberry at them from underneath my yashmak and left, to exclamations of 'How extraordinary!' from John and 'Bloody rude, if you ask me!' from Wilfrid.

Marrakesh was a city of extremes: the contrast between the poor and the so-called élite was appalling. I felt shame living in the luxury of the hotel, when outside the gates at all hours were beggars, street vendors, crippled children in rags being pushed forward by their elders to beg. One morning as I was leaving the hotel I was horrified by the sight of two Moroccan men holding out a dead baby to me. They were wailing something I couldn't understand, obviously asking me for money to bury the poor little thing. I was so upset that I ran away in tears. When I arrived at the location site the first person I saw was Wilfrid.

'My dear girl, whatever is the matter?' he asked, shocked at seeing me in such distress. I sobbed out my story. There was a long pause. 'Oh dear me,' said Wilfrid. 'For sale, I suppose.'

His outrageous remark had the desired effect and I started to laugh. He then mitigated his seeming heartlessness by pointing out that the poor little soul was probably in better hands now than it had been in when alive.

During our stay in Marrakesh John and I hired a bicycle each. I explored the city on mine, while John would wobble off to the location on his. He would set off amid the traffic dressed in a city suit, pinstriped trousers and a bowler hat, oblivious of the attention he attracted among the Arabs in their flowing robes. 'Do get in the car and go to work in the proper manner, Johnny,' Wilfrid would say as he set out. But John stuck to his bike right to the last.

We never lost touch with Willy, as John affectionately called him. So often when working on films you meet people with whom you get on, swear undying friendship, only to lose touch once the film is over, but in Willy's case John and I always looked him up whenever he was working in England. And we always laughed over our shared memories of Marrakesh.

Over the years John and I spent more and more time in Ramsgate. John had a love–hate relationship with the place, but there was something womblike about it that appealed to him. He slowly dug himself in and became part of the scenery as far as the local people were concerned. He certainly knew all the local gossip, gleaned on his twice-daily visits to the local pub, and he would often bring back titbits of information.

One day he came home chuckling to himself. On his way back from the pub he had passed a group of people and heard one of them, say, 'Oh look, there's Sergeant Wilson from *The Army Game*.' People getting his name or the name of the show wrong always irritated him, so as he passed he drew in his stomach and let his pants fall down. Luckily he had timed his protest so that it took place just by our front gate, so he was able to make a quick escape into the house, followed by cries of 'Oo-er, did you see that?'

On another occasion a television repair man came to fix our set. 'You'll never guess who I've just seen,' he said to me. 'That chap from *Dad's Army*, Sergeant Wilson. He must be stinking rich, the old bugger.'

'What makes you say that?' I asked, feigning ignorance.

'Well, because he's such a scruffy old sod. He obviously doesn't care what he looks like.'

At that moment John walked in. 'Ah, well done,' he said, 'Just in time for the race meeting.'

Dad's Army was fast becoming one of the most popular comedy shows on television and cast and wives alike became a close-knit group of friends. Jimmy Beck, who played the spiv, and John became inseparable, and most days Jimmy would come home with John after work for a drink and a chat. On Friday nights all the wives would meet at the BBC for the transmission of the show. Jim's wife Kay and Clive Dunn's wife, the actress Cilla Morgan, and I were particularly close friends, and we usually had dinner together after the show.

Clive, Cilla, John and I went on holiday together to Portugal. We rented a luxury villa between us, complete with swimming pool, tennis court and a large vegetable garden where we could pick fresh produce for dinner every night. One evening John was lying reading on a sun bed by the pool and the rest of us were sitting on the terrace. 'Would you like a drink?' I called.

'Oh, how lovely,' said John, and rolled languidly into the swimming pool fully dressed. He was still wearing his watch.

Dinny had taught John how to do prattfalls, and the exhibitionist in him couldn't resist trying them out in the weirdest cicumstances. He suddenly did one on the bar of the Bell Hotel, Thetford, where most of the exteriors of *Dad's Army* were filmed. It was at the end of a busy day's work and all the cast and crew were present. John said the different reactions were most interesting. One of the make-up girls, who had a bit of a crush on him, fell to her knees and cradled his head in her lap. Jimmy Perry and David Croft, the scriptwriters, turned pale, probably at the thought of all the rewrites, and Bill Pertwee told him not to be an idiot.

It was while we were on holiday with the Dunns in

Portugal for the second time that we received a telegram telling us of the tragic death of Jimmy Beck. Poor Jimmy, he was just beginning to get his foot on the ladder to stardom, having been given his own series. He was a fine actor, and sadly missed by John. I'll never forget the courage of his wife Kay, who sat by his bed as he lay in a coma for three weeks, knowing that he would never pull through but hoping for a miracle.

After we had lived in Ramsgate for five years, we decided to buy a bigger house. Rather I decided, and then persuaded John that it would be a good investment. Left to his own devices the idea of taking the trouble to invest in anything would never have occurred to him. He wasn't really interested in money. Of course, he wanted to have enough of the stuff to enable him to live the sort of life he was accustomed to, but if he had earned millions he would not have changed his way of life by one iota. We didn't have a car – he had stopped driving when the Breathalyser test came in – and if we needed to go anywhere we would hire a mini cab. When it came to clothes, John would make the odd excursion to Turnbull and Asser for shirts and to Simpson's for jackets, and that was that. He knew exactly what he wanted, and the speed with which he entered and left the premises was nothing short of mercurial. 'I'll have this jacket,' he would say to the assistant, picking the most expensive cashmere from the rack. He never asked the price. In the shoe department he gave the same performance. 'Those shoes in my size?' he would say, and somehow they always seemed to fit. He would then rush off to the nearest bar, leaving me to pay and wait for the goods to be wrapped. Therefore when it came to the purchase of another house, John once again left everything to me. As before, he moved in only when all the alterations had been completed and his armchair was in place in front of the fire.

It was a happy house. John and I each had a large double bedroom overlooking the garden with its flowering cherry trees. My father loved growing things and under his tuition I became a gardening fanatic. I turned a large part over to vegetables and planted potatoes, carrots, onions, beans, beets, greens and salad stuffs. The thrill of digging up my first potatoes of the year and serving them steamed, with home-grown mint and parsley butter, was unsurpassed. I started a herb garden and learned about drying and using herbs for teas and health aids. Then I bought a greenhouse and began growing plants from seed.

Unable to bring any enthusiasm to bear on the whole venture, John would watch apologetically while I laboured away at the compost heap. 'Do you really like doing this?' he once asked me as, sweating with exertion, I clumped up from the garden in my mud-encrusted wellies to join him where he sat in his peacock chair on the patio. 'It makes me feel guilty just watching you.'

For the umpteenth time I assured him that I loved doing it and that it would do him no harm if he did a little gardening himself.

He shuddered. 'I'm sorry, darling, but I think it's ghastly,' he said.

Lots of people came to stay with us. Annie Ross was a regular visitor. Being a gourmet cook, she was wild about all my compost-grown vegetables and loved taking things fresh from the ground for dinner. Annie has a sense of wonder about her, in spite of the fact that she has done so many things. She was a child star in Hollywood at the same time as Judy Garland and Shirley Temple. She made her name as a jazz singer in the famous trio of Lambert Hendricks and Ross who had their own unique style of scat singing. She has performed in cabaret and is also an actress of some note. In fact, she is just about the most sophisticated person I know. But how she enjoyed digging up a root of spuds or weeding a flowerbed. And always after dinner and a couple of glasses of wine we would do our harmony act from *House of Flowers*.

Mark was another regular visitor. He and John were close friends by then, and none of us thought it odd that he spent so much of his free time with us. Over the years he brought lots of different girlfriends down to meet us but when he turned up with Diana it was easy to see that she was something special, both in herself and in terms of his feelings towards her. John and I fell in love with her on sight. 'Can we keep this one in the family?' I asked Mark, and we did. I was happy and proud to be matron-of-honour at their wedding at Caxton Hall. We had a field day with the reporters when it came to explaining who we all were, because Diana's first husband was also there with their son Saul; then there was David, and also Polly, Mark and Diana's daughter, who had been born before their marriage. I thank Mark for many things, but especially for bringing Diana into my life. She has turned out to be the best and dearest friend I have ever had.

Over the years I settled more and more happily into my life with John. I don't say that I didn't have a few adventures – I was left alone a lot of the time and knowing Tony had given me a taste for passion and drama. But none of my affairs was the slightest threat to my marriage. John also had the odd indiscretion. Women were often attracted to him but they always had to make the advances. He was so polite that he really didn't like to refuse anyone. He always told me about his adventures, and I understood, knowing that they were merely passing fancies. If we could come through my affair with Tony, I reckoned that we could weather just about anything.

Indeed, there was one occasion that John told me about which made me gasp at the boldness of some women. At the time John was touring with *Dad's Army*, and one night after the show he went with some of the cast to a drinking club. A rather attractive middle-aged woman attached herself to him. She told him that she was a sister at the local hospital, and at the end of the evening she offered to give him a lift home in her car. Unsuspecting, John accepted. When he got in the car and settled himself beside her, she turned on the cassette machine and played him a tape of very explicit pornography. After it had finished they sat in silence for some time. Suddenly she said, 'I'd like to be fucked in a ditch.'

John cleared his throat. 'Well, my dear, I'd like to oblige you,' he said, 'but it's rather late and dark, and I really can't see myself clambering about at this time of night looking for a ditch. Perhaps we ought to do it by daylight.'

She never took him up on his invitation, much to his relief.

It was typical of John to tell me about that incident. And typical of me to keep my escapades to myself. I saw no point in shaking John's security – he had been through enough uncertainty already.

Over the years, when he was busy learning his lines, John would ask me to read his scripts. One day he received a script written by Dennis Potter. Entitled *Traitor*, it was based on the life of Kim Philby. It was a jewel of a part, the best thing that John had ever been asked to do. Naturally, I was very excited about it. 'This is the one, John,' I said. 'This is important.'

Now, like all true Arians, John could be very contrary, and I had learned that the best way to spark his interest in something was for me to appear to dislike or disapprove of it. However, such was my enthusiasm for *Traitor*, I quite forgot to use this ploy, with the result that I had to work hard to convince him to do it. 'Too many words' was one excuse. 'Too much strain' was another. 'It will be forgotten a week after I've done it,' he said.

But it wasn't forgotten, because John won the BAFTA award for the best actor of 1971 for that effort, and quite an effort it was. As soon as he had accepted the part we went down to Ramsgate, where he spent the three weeks before the first rehearsal swotting up his lines. He worked in his room all day, and in the evening I would listen to him going through them over and over again, until by the first rehearsal he had the part under his hat.

When we heard that he had been nominated for best actor, he was working in Bristol starring in a series called

A Class of His Own about an impoverished peer trying to turn his crumbling stately home into a rather tatty Longleat. The BAFTA representative rang me in London and asked me to make sure John was at the Albert Hall on award night. I pointed out that he would have to leave Bristol straight after work and leave London immediately after the award ceremony in order to be back in Bristol ready for work the following morning; I was reluctant to make him rush about like that unless he had won. The BAFTA man told me that John had indeed won but asked me not to tell him as they wanted the announcement to come as a surprise to him on the night.

I tried to keep it a secret, but John suspected from my face that the prize was his. On the journey to the Albert Hall I kept trying to fob him off, but when we arrived we were given such deferential treatment and were seated at a table near the stage that he knew he had won. Nevertheless, it was a thrill when his name was called and he went to receive his prize.

Earlier that same evening, while John was travelling up from Bristol, the phone had rung, and a man's voice had said, 'Are you sitting down, Mrs Le Mesurier, because we have a wonderful surprise for you? We want to do *This Is Your Life* on John.' I replied that I had a very happy marriage and wanted to keep it that way, and that I had promised my husband under threat of divorce that I would never let *This Is Your Life* happen to him. The man did his best to persuade me but I refused to budge. Eventually John's agent at the time, a wonderfully urbane man called Freddy Joachim, managed to convince the producer that John would not agree. It is something I now regret because I feel that deep down he probably *would* have liked to have been the subject of the programme. There's not an actor alive who doesn't like to have his ego stroked from time to time, and John was no exception. It would also have been something to treasure after he died.

Just after the success of *Traitor* BOAC, as it was then called, asked John to make some commercials about a rather vague Englishman getting into a muddle at airports and being helped through them by the service and civility of BOAC. With my fear of flying, I elected not to accompany him as usual. His agent Peter Campbell, who took over when Freddy retired, went instead. John gave me such a glowing account of his travels, particularly his time in Hong Kong, that when he was to return to Australia to do a tour of major cities, the commercial having been such a success, I plucked up my courage and went with him.

We arrived in Sydney in pouring rain, our ankles were swollen and our time clocks working backwards. BOAC had laid on a press conference for John at the airport. Peter and I sat at the back of the room and watched. The journalists were very pushy. One young woman asked John how much he was earning on the tour, and John replied that that was none of her business. On our way to the hotel we were accompanied by a PR man who seemed rather overawed by John. Uncharacteristically John began to complain about having to be subjected to a press conference as soon as he stepped off the plane. 'I'm sure Robert Morley didn't have to put up with this sort of thing in America,' he said.

'Come on, John, that's what we're here for,' I said wearily from the back of the car.

The PR man told me afterwards that he had indeed been absolutely terrified of John, and when he heard me pipe up from the back he breathed a sigh of relief.

Now I wasn't unaware of the fact that visiting the city where Tony had died might be a depressing experience, but I wasn't prepared for what happened to me when I entered the hotel bedroom. As I started to unpack a feeling of such black despair came over me that I had an insane desire to throw myself out of the bedroom window. I sat on the bed and burst into uncontrollable sobs. There suddenly seemed no hope in the world, no point in living. I was shaking with panic and John could get no sense out of me. My behaviour distressed him terribly, but I was unable to stop. He rang Peter's room and asked for help, but Peter had never seen me carry on like this before and was just as perplexed as John. They were afraid to leave me alone for fear that I might do something silly, so although it was the middle of the morning, they gave me two sleeping pills and stayed with me until I fell asleep. While I was sleeping a room-service waiter who worked on our floor jumped to his death from a window. He crashed through an awning and a glass roof and landed among the guests having lunch in the restaurant.

I slept all that day and all the next night without stirring, and when I woke up the next morning I was back to normal. I can't explain my mood. Perhaps the waiter had been in our room just before we arrived and I had picked up his vibrations or perhaps it was the thought of Tony – he may have stayed in the same hotel: it was more likely – or perhaps it was just the effects of jet lag. I had suffered bouts of depression before, but they had never affected me in that way.

The next day we moved to a small family hotel on Bondi Beach and my depression passed. I resolved that I would put Tony out of my mind completely and not go in search of the house where he died or make inquiries about him. It would have been unfair to John, and I knew that, wherever Tony's spirit was, it certainly wouldn't be hanging around in Sydney. Instead I threw myself into seeing as much of that wonderful city as I could.

The sheer colour of Australia left me speechless. The birds were like great glamorous versions of our own species – huge green thrushes and bright, blazing blue blackbirds. There were flocks of parakeets and cockatoos and I heard the deep laugh of the kookaburra. I held a koala bear and a baby possum, and gasped at the richness of it all. I tried to swim off Bondi Beach, but the surf was so strong that I ended up bare-arsed with my bikini bottom wrapped around my ankles, so I stuck to the shark-free safety of swimming pools after that.

After Sydney we visited all the big cities and in each one John was interviewed within an inch of his life for television and radio and by countless journalists. What he hadn't grasped was that BOAC wanted him to promote winter holidays in England and when a TV chat-show host in Brisbane asked him what England was like at this time of the year, he replied, 'Oh, it's absolutely ghastly. I wouldn't advise anyone to go there now. May is rather pleasant, but at the moment we're in the grip of winter, and when we left there were tanks all around the edge of the airport watching for terrorists.' At the back of the studio Peter and I tried to smother our giggles.

'Have you picked up any of our colloquialisms?' asked another interviewer.

'"Rooting" seems to be a widely used expression out here,' said John looking straight at the camera, knowing full well that in Australia 'rooting' means having sex. A roar of laughter went up from the sound box and Peter and I gasped at his audacity. But John always knew how to behave outrageously and get away with it. He relied on his deceptive air of innocence.

We covered Adelaide, Perth, Hobart and Melbourne, where Peter left us for home. We returned to Sydney alone for the last week of the tour. We had been paid handsomely for that wonderful experience and decided to spend our expenses money on stopping off in Fiji and Los Angeles on the way home. There is a legend that God had made just one place in the world perfect as an example to the rest of us, and that place was Fiji. If I had thought Australia colourful, it paled into nothing against Fiji. There were flamboyant trees, bigger than English oaks, covered in bright red flowers. There were flowers of every hue, size, shape and perfume wherever I looked. When I put my head under the crystal clear water the colour went right on blazing. There were jellyfish like bunches of blue wistaria with tiny fish all shades of the rainbow darting among them. One evening, as we were driving back to the hotel, the sunset was at its most potent, the sky a rich mixture of red and purple streaks. We turned a corner and there was a lake of white waterlilies, turned pink by the sunset, and, riding naked and bareback on wild horses, three Fijian children with frangipani blossoms in their hair. We both gasped. 'It's all a little bit over the top, isn't it?' said John, ever one for understatement.

After Fiji, Los Angeles looked like an unfinished building site, but John, with his love of movies, was fascinated by it. We saw all the obligatory tourist sights, including Gruman's Chinese Theatre, and stood at the corner of Hollywood and Vine. We also went to Chasons, where Cubby Broccolli recognized John and came over to our table, which pleased John quite a bit.

When we returned to England we felt we had been on the trip of a lifetime.

In 1976 John was approached by a man who was to become a very close friend. Derek Taylor had been the Beatles' press officer for many years, and was managing director of Warner Brothers Records in England. He and John met while they were recording the cast album for the stage musical of *Dad's Army* and, as Derek said, they connected.

For me, and for many others, one of the most magical moments of the show was when John, all alone on the stage, sang 'A Nightingale Sang in Berkeley Square'. It was a wistful, tender moment and it was always greeted by thunderous applause. John's performance gave Derek the idea they should make an album. So they put their heads together and came up with a jewel of a record. It was beautifully produced and has proved to be enduring: it can never go out of fashion in this disposable age. Derek gave John a free hand to chose his own guests. John invited Annie Ross and a wonderful pianist and old friend, Alan Clare, to take part. Then between them Derek and John selected the rest of the material. Their similar tastes and attitudes made the task easy. They used some Noël Coward and readings from Steven Leacock – a firm favourite of them both (and incidentally, of Tony, who bought me a book of Leacock's essays and could never read them out to me for laughing). John sang 'Nightingale' to the accompaniment of a vast string orchestra and – to fill a gap – suggested an extract from my favourite book, *Cider with Rosie* by Laurie Lee.

Making the album with Derek gave John more pleasure than anything he had ever done before. Although it didn't make much money, it became something of a collectors' item and he received fan letters from people all over the world. To round it off John had chosen a Red Indian prayer which he had been asked to read at a friend's memorial service. It was so appropriate that I asked for it to be played at John's funeral service, so that John's own voice read the words that captured exactly the way he himself had felt.

When I am dead cry for me a little.
Think of me sometimes
but not too much.

Think of me now and again as I was in life,
at some moment it is pleasant to recall.
But not for long.

Leave me in peace, and I shall leave you in peace,
and while you live let your thoughts be with the living.

After working together so closely on the album, John and Derek formed a bond that was never broken. They met often during the following years and began writing to each other on a regular basis. Derek's letters were a joy – John would read them over and over again and when the family came to stay, Derek's latest letters were obligatory after-dinner entertainment. I have kept them all. They cheered John up and made him laugh right up to the end, when there wasn't much left to laugh about.

Sixteen

In 1977 John was invited back to Australia to star in a Molière play, _The Miser_. We were both elated at the opportunity to see Australia again, although John groaned a bit at the choice of play, never being overly enthusiastic about the classics, apart from Ibsen and Chekhov, both of whose works suited his vague, remote style.

John elected to go ahead of me. He preferred to be alone during the rehearsal period, doing little else but work, learn his lines and sleep. I always felt in the way, which indeed I was. I was more use once the play got underway, giving him the encouragement he so badly needed and seeing that his wants were attended to.

He phoned me a few times while he was rehearsing. On each occasion he said that he regretted not taking me with him from the start. He complained a lot, which was unlike him, and said that there was a lack of rapport between him arfd the Australian cast. He also said that the heat was bothering him and that he was constantly exhausted.

All this was so worrying that I wanted to join him earlier than we had arranged, but John was always superstitious about changing plans and insisted that I hang on and arrive in time for his opening night.

The day of my departure arrived. David, who was by then living permanently in London, had arranged to come with me to Heathrow. We had rung for a car and were waiting in the hall with our coats on, when Peter Campbell rang. 'Thank God I caught you before you left for the airport,' he said. He had just that moment heard that John had collapsed during the dress rehearsal and had been rushed to hospital. He was apparently suffering from exhaustion. I was told to stay put as he would be coming home as soon as he was fit enough to travel.

The shock of this news floored me completely. My first instinct was to go to him, but Peter pointed out that by the time I arrived the powers-that-be would have him on a plane and on his way home. Further calls to Australia confirmed that John wanted me to stay in England, and a few days later I met him at Heathrow.

I received an even greater shock when I saw him. He was in a wheelchair looking desperately ill. He seemed to have aged ten years in the few weeks he had been away and I was hard pressed to hold back the tears.

As soon as we got back to the flat he went straight to bed. 'I've been longing for this moment,' he said, and immediately fell into a deep relaxed sleep.

The next morning the doctor came to see him. He diagnosed depression and prescribed antidepressants. However, he didn't give John a thorough examination. I said that I thought John was only depressed because he was ill, to which the doctor replied that he was ill because he was depressed. Giving the doctor the benefit of the doubt, I gave John two of the prescribed pills, with the result that the following day he was semi-conscious. I threw the rest of the pills down the lavatory. When the effect of the dose had worn off and John was able to walk, we decided to go to Ramsgate as quickly as possible. We both needed the comfort and security of our real home, the sea air, and the cats we loved, and the down-to-earth support of my parents to still our fears about what John's illness might be.

As soon as we arrived in Ramsgate I rang our family doctor, who came immediately and diagnosed a serious liver problem. The following day John was admitted to Ramsgate hospital, where the consultant confirmed that he was suffering from cirrhosis of the liver.

There was no treatment, just total abstinence from alcohol and bed rest. John was warned that to go on drinking would prove fatal. I asked about a special diet and was told to give him anything he fancied. I did, with dire results.

I studied my health-food books: raw fruit and salads were recommended. John would have nothing to do with them, so I called in a naturopath, who, after examining John, walked me around the garden and told me that unless I took his advice my husband would die quite soon. Raw fruit for one month, then on to raw vegetables and salads. He wasn't even to drink tea or coffee. I asked the naturopath to tell John himself what he had told me. This he did, adding that even smoking was damaging John's liver. John moaned, but I had the upper hand.

The next examination at the hospital amazed the specialist. John's liver was mending. He was out of danger, but so weak he could hardly walk unaided. He was as thin as a stick, and his eyes were great sunken hollows in his craggy face. People who came to visit were shocked at his appearance.

Gradually he regained his strength and I was able to introduce other foods into his diet. But how he missed his booze. Hattie sent down bottles of non-alcoholic wine, but he said it tasted like grape juice. He was miserable and wouldn't let go of his craving for alcohol. During the following year, as he regained his strength, his need for a drink increased. He felt foolish going to the local pub and toying with a lemonade. Peter Campbell often came down to see him, as did Mark, Diana and the children. All of them were concerned about the way he looked and his general air of dejection.

He made another six episodes of *Dad's Army*. Although working again was good therapy, it was a mistake. He looked so ill that the public thought he was on his last legs, and the press came down to Ramsgate to take photographs of him at home to prove that he was still alive and kicking. However, for a long time afterwards there were few offers of work, as he was considered a bad risk by the insurance companies. We ran out of money and had to sell the London flat, which was a wrench, especially for John, as he was more of a city person than I was. We sold at a considerable loss, having, with immaculate timing, missed the London property boom.

People thought that John was incredibly rich because his face appeared in so many films. What they didn't understand was that he often worked for just one day in cameo roles which paid very little, so although he had a face that was recognized all over the world, he certainly didn't have a hefty regular income.

We were certainly not on the breadline but to compensate for being out of work John began to toy with the idea of writing his autobiography. It wasn't until the last year of his life that anything came of it, when it was published under the title *A Jobbing Actor*. At the time it was something to occupy him during the long months without work.

By now David was living with a girl whom he had met when he was a mature sixteen year old. In those days Susie was a top model, a fairy princess of a girl, blonde and petite, but smart and very practical. David said that whenever he looked at her it was like having an eyebath. They are still together, and Susie has blessed me with a granddaughter Emma, a replica of herself.

So now Ramsgate was our only home, and because of that we had company most weekends. Peter was the most frequent visitor. He was also Annie Ross's agent, and it was after one of Peter's weekend visits that Annie rang to tell me that John was having a drink from time to time. He had sworn poor Peter to secrecy, putting him in the unenviable position of either being a snitch or helping his friend and client do something that would ultimately kill him. In desperation Peter had taken Annie into his confidence, and she of course rang me.

I asked our family doctor to explain in vivid detail the harm that John was doing by continuing to drink with a damaged liver. After his lecture, all was well for a while, then John began to come home from his lunchtime lemonade smelling strongly of mints. It amazed me that, after he had been so ill although he had been told that to go on drinking would prove fatal, he still refused to stop. After all, it wasn't as if he changed at all after a drink, like Tony had done. If anything he just became a little more morose. It was a side of John's character that I never understood.

I tried everything to get him to stop. I even threatened to divorce him on the grounds that I couldn't bear to watch him doing something that would take him away from me. But John, for all his gentleness, was stubborn. I became a sort of minder, refusing to let him out of my sight. I nagged, pleaded and wept.

We called a family conference. David and Susie, Peter, Mum and Dad. I pleaded my case, then John pleaded his. He argued that it was, after all, *his* life, and without the normality of being able to have a drink when he fancied one, meet up with his mates in London from time to time and have a drink with them on an equal footing, then he would just as soon be dead. He said that he loved me and our life together, but for the past year and a half he had been unhappy. He preferred quality to quantity. He promised to drink nothing but beer, and that in moderation, but he was incapable of giving up alcohol completely. I was out-voted. I gave up. All I could do was treasure each day with him from then on.

The funny thing was that as soon as beer was back on his diet, he started to put on weight, the colour came back to his face, he was happy, and work started to flow his way again.

We shared almost six good years together, years in which he did some of his best work. They were quality years of a good vintage, during which he drank moderately. We were closer than ever, and happier. His illness had been a sharp reminder of the impermanence of things.

During the last two years of John's life, everything started to go bad. My father became ill with cancer and I went through the ordeal of seeing him deteriorate. Then many of John's friends died, beginning with Hattie's

217

sudden death – there was Peter Sellers, Bill Evans, Seth Holt, David Niven, Arthur Lowe.

John began to have nightmares. He came into my bedroom early morning white and trembling after a vivid dream in which Arthur had appeared and said cheerfully, 'Come on, Johnny, we're all waiting for you. Don't tell Joanie.' He had woken up in a sweat of fear and gone downstairs. It was only about six o'clock on a fine summer morning. He opened the french windows and a blackbird hopped into the room. I went cold when he told me, but tried to shrug it off as superstition.

Some three weeks later at about six o'clock in the morning John began to haemorrhage. I called the ambulance and he was admitted once more to Ramsgate hospital. The consultant managed to stop the bleeding, but warned me that it might happen again. I didn't know then that it was the beginning of the end.

After a week John was discharged. He was put on a salt-free diet and told to rest as much as possible. There was no treatment. In my innocence I believed that the haemorrhage had been a warning, that all he had to do was stop drinking, which this time he did, and that everything would be all right.

We were closer than ever after that scare. I went everywhere with him, not that he could go very far – a short walk along the cliffs was all that he could manage. I had alerted his sons Robin and Kim when he had been taken ill. Kim often came down to see him. Robin, who was by then a guitarist in Rod Stewart's band, was touring in the Far East but kept in close touch.

A month later it happened again. This time Mark was there, and once again it started early in the morning. This time I knew that John was terminally ill. I sat outside the ward while the hospital staff attempted to arrest the bleeding and gave way to deepest despair.

The consultant decided that John would be better off at King's Hospital. Mark, David and I followed the ambulance to London.

By the time I was allowed to see John the bleeding had stopped and he was in a deep coma. The doctor told me that he might be able to hear me, but that he could be unconscious for forty-eight hours. I held his hand and bent over him. 'If you can hear me, John, squeeze my hand,' I whispered in his ear. His fingers tightened around mine. 'Now, John,' I said firmly, 'you are in London in the best hospital in Europe. You are out of danger and all you have to do is relax and rest.'

Very softly he whispered, 'National Health?'

'Yes,' I replied.

'Thank God,' he murmured, and fell asleep.

During that period in London Mark and Diana were my salvation. They drove me to and from the hospital every day, kept my spirits up and my sense of humour intact. It was during this period that Diana brought Canon Gerry Parrott into my life, on a morning when my sense of humour had slipped away, leaving me face to face with things as they were. I was having a confidential weep in the kitchen before going to the hospital, when Diana suddenly said, 'There's somebody I want you to meet.' On the way to Southwark Cathedral where he worked she told me about him. Knowing her views on organized religion, her attitude surprised me. I had in my mind's eye a picture of an elderly cleric, so it came as a pleasant surprise to be introduced to a handsome man with thick, prematurely white hair, twinkling blue eyes that reminded me of David Niven, and a smile that reached into the dusty corners of my soul. Over a drink and a sandwich I found a friend for life and beyond. Once again fate had stepped in and given me a helper. Gerry Parrott radiated positive energy and, along with Mark and Diana, provided the support I needed to get me through that awful time.

After two weeks at King's Hospital John was discharged. By then it was early September. He had first fallen ill on 5 July; two months had passed and my life, along with many false values, had completely changed.

For the next two months, apart from one more brief

return to King's for tests, John was at home. He was now on a rigid diet; not a trace of salt was allowed. I found it difficult to keep his tastebuds alive and began to experiment with herbs and other flavourings to add to his food. I decided I would try to write a salt-free cookery book, as at that time there wasn't one in existence. It was good therapy for me, and John, who had never shown much interest in food before, became quite involved in my culinary skills. However it came to nothing as at the time John was still working on the completion of *Jobbing Actor* which sadly he never saw published. I lived from hour to hour, trying to remain totally in the present and not allow my mind to wander beyond the next meal, the day's television programmes, his book and the blessed garden, which provided me with the means to keep fit and busy. Company came – Gerry Parrott, Mark and Diana, Peter Campbell – but John was tiring more and more and sleeping for longer periods.

Early in November he started to haemorrhage again. The ambulance took him from me for the last time. David and Kim came down to say goodbye and Robin was notified. There was nothing to be done, except pray that he would make a good end. I had been warned that death from liver failure could be awful. Prayer was all that was left.

It was impossible to move him from the main ward of Ramsgate hospital to a private room – he was too ill and had to be constantly under observation. There was a serious lack of nurses and conditions were pretty dire. I stayed with him every day and helped nurse him myself, only being thrown out when a consultant appeared.

As we lived only yards from the hospital I could pop home at any time and cook something special if John had a fancy to eat anything, but in the end I was using the house only for sleeping and bathing. I would spend the entire day at the hospital. By then he was very weak, slipping in and out of consciousness. I still talked as if he were suffering from a passing illness that simply had to be endured; John didn't want to know the true nature of his illness.

On the Saturday before he died the television set at the end of the ward showed *Where the Spies Are*, a film in which he appeared with David Niven. He had been working on it when I first started my affair with Tony, and it was painful and eerie to see John on the screen looking so handsome and healthy, while in reality he was lying in that ghastly ward so close to death.

Just before the end Mark and Diana came to see him. We knew that he hadn't long to go – he was very weak, but still in possession of his senses. As Mark leaned over him, John took his hand. 'Hello, my dear fellow,' he said. 'I see you've grown a beard.'

'Yes, I'm doing *Educating Rita*,' said Mark, 'playing the professor, and I thought it might help me look more intelligent.'

'And has it?' said John with a twinkle in his eye. It was his last joke.

Later that day he said to me, 'Darling, I'm fed up of it now and I think I'd like to die.' He held tightly to my hand and said, 'It's all been rather lovely,' and within an hour he had slipped into a coma.

Being 'fed up of it' came from one of Clive and Cilla Dunn's children. Apparently she became bored during a matinée at the theatre and in the middle of a very dramatic silence said very loudly, 'I'm fed up of it now. I want to go home.' That phrase became part of our vocabulary, so I suppose it was appropriate that John would use it when he was 'fed up of' life.

He never regained consciousness. When his breathing stopped a few minutes later, I saw him quite clearly in my mind's eye ambling towards the light. I knew that Tony would be the first to welcome him.

Later that day when the clan gathered in Ramsgate, we resolved to honour his wish that on the day he died the following announcement would appear in the obituary column of *The Times*:

221

John Le Mesurier wishes it to be known that he 'conked out' on November 15th.

He sadly misses family and friends.

That obituary was taken up by the press and appeared on the billboards all over the country. That evening the newsreaders on all the television channels quoted it, so even the sadness of his passing was tempered by laughter.

His funeral was attended by the people whom John loved. It was a carefully planned tribute to his well-lived life, unique as funerals go because lightness and laughter were the keynotes. John would have hated tears at his last gathering. At times the church rang with laughter. The people waiting in the anteroom for the next service must have wondered what was going on.

The service was conducted by Canon Gerry Parrott, and Bill Pertwee, who played the air-raid warden in *Dad's Army*, spoke with tenderness and humour about the years that they worked together. Derek Taylor wrote the following tribute, which was read by Mark:

The many writers and broadcasters who have expressed themselves on John's 'conking out' have found themselves unable to separate their love for the *idea* of the man from their appreciation of his art.

A leader in *The Guardian* said: 'The character he cumulatively created will be remembered when others more famous are forgotten not just for the skill of his playing but because he somehow embodied a symbolic British reaction to the whirlpool of the modern world – endlessly perplexed by the dizzying and incoherent pattern of events but doing his courteous best to ensure that resentment never showed.'

As Max Miller said of himself, 'There'll never be another' and there hasn't been and won't be, so *we* say of John: 'There'll never be another' and there cannot be. He was his own marvellous invention, a man of his time and up with the times, and not as puzzled as he pretended, in fact a man who missed very little but, dissembling beautifully, concealed with great restraint what Philip French in *The Observer* newspaper has called 'a reserve of kindness and a strong vein of malice'.

His private humour was strong in irony and biting asides and he liked to read of it in others. In a letter to me (one of scores to brighten my mornings) he quoted James Agate: 'Mrs Pat, terribly bored by an elderly scientist drooling on and on about ants: "They are wonderful little creatures and they have their own police force and their own army." She leaned forward with an expression of the utmost interest and in a voice like damson-coloured velvet said: "No navy, I suppose".'

He wrote once from the north: 'Here I am in glorious Leeds. It is Sunday evening as I write and it's pissing down outside. I am here to appear on somebody else's programme. Top whack is £200, and getting to and from here and staying in the railway hotel I will no doubt arrive back in Ramsgate with ten shillings.'

In another letter he enclosed an early picture of Mabel and Wilfred Pickles: 'Two people to be really proud of.' He wrote: 'The kind of example they set and the entertainment they served to millions is surely something to cherish.'

And again: 'I went to see a tightly corseted Prussian general who works under the name of Otto Preminger . . . I put down on his desk a book about Ronnie Scott's club . . . Preminger picked it up, sniffed at it and asked if it was a present for him. I said: "Well no, not really." On his handing it back to me I found myself saying: "Perhaps *Tales from the Vienna Woods* might be more suitable." '

Writing of a fellow actor of some conceit, he said: 'Given to wearing Anderson and Shepherd suits, full of charm and haughtiness, he is convinced he is thirteenth or fourteenth in line to the throne.'

When John was chosen to play Gandalf in *Lord of the Rings* on BBC Radio, he wrote: 'It is a bit too fey for me and I do not understand it too well. But I have friends like Michael Hordern, Ian Holm and Robert Stephens in it – they don't understand it either.'

In a reference to a voice-over he said: 'I was due to do a Cadbury commercial but at the last moment it was cancelled because the product became inedible and in fact tasted like an ageing turd . . . So it's back to the drawing board or the labs again so that the commodity can be made more enchanting. I laugh about these things sometimes but not always.'

In the *Observer* Philip French wrote: 'He could be very funny and very sad.' It was this ambivalence that bound me to him with hoops of steel. He knew that life could be bloody, knew that it *was*, but like those bad films among the good in which he appeared as that jobbing actor, there was always the shining Le Mesurier moment when things didn't seem quite so ghastly after all.

Things did happen to him. He told me once he had, that very week, seen a hen fall over as it walked down a lane. 'Not an everyday sight,' he said. He wrote to me from London in 1980: 'At 3 a.m. the bell rang and there was someone breathing heavily through the letter box saying that he had met me in Tregunter Road, Earls Court, in 1950 and had something he wanted to show me. We called the police and sent him merrily on his way.'

Just recently, after coming out of hospital, he wrote of walking to the local pub for a lemonade or bitter lemon. 'People are very kind and thoughtful,' he said, 'and tell me how pleased they are to see me "about again" and then proceed to give me a blow by blow account of their *own* ailments. All of which is not too riveting but "well meant", as my mother used to say. I tend to think twice before venturing out too far without Joan near at hand. She has been marvellous throughout all this carry on, helpful and patient.'

He achieved more than he knew. He had become not just a good man, but a great one and it has been reflected these last days in a torrent of obituary quite without precedent for anyone other than a knight of the theatre or a world star. 'No wonder,' *The Guardian* leader said, 'that so many whose lives were very different from his own came to be so enormously fond of him.' We, his friends, who knew and loved him in our ways offer his dear family our thanks for sharing such a man with us in such generous measure.

I could go on about the many blessings John gave me. Robin and Kim, the two sons from his marriage to Hattie, are as close to me as my own son David. They have adopted me as a sort of surrogate mother and I am now the senior member of the family. Imagine that . . . Where did all the years go?

Epilogue

Sitges is beautiful at this time of year. Spring comes early. It is mid-February, the mimosa is in full power and the almond trees are covered in blossom. There is a lot of green about. Come summer it will have retreated from the full force of the sun and the landscape will be barren and baked.

It is during July and August that I miss England, when the heat seems to draw the breath out of me and makes the simplest tasks into massive obstacles. My fourth summer in Spain is approaching. John has been dead over four years now, and Dad three.

My mother divides her time between Sitges and Ramsgate, and I have replaced my tiny cottage by a huge casa. Its tiled floors, old beams and cool white walls are spread over four levels. Mark made me buy it. He and many of my friends used to come and stay in the cottage, and Mark finally decided that I needed somewhere bigger. He helped me out financially and a few other friends chipped in, with the result that I am running a sort of time-share mansion which has provided me with a beautiful home and plenty of company.

Emma often comes to stay. She is almost eight now, and to her Sitges is a paradise on earth. We live thirty yards from the sea, and the same distance from the rocks beneath the church where the feral cats live.

I have taken it upon myself to care for them. The locals and my friends call me the cat lady, but the animals and their needs have given me a purpose and routine. Two of them have moved in with me. I took them from the rocks when they were poor things, half dead from cat flu, promising myself that I would return them to the wild when they were strong, but when the time came I was unable to put them back. They are exquisite lionesses now, still untamed and fiercely territorial, but not averse to being stroked or creeping into bed with me on cold mornings.

What a life-change there has been. How winding the road that has brought me here. Or was it, perhaps, that I was heading in this direction all the time?

In the past I probably believed I knew the score while I was frantically searching for answers from different religions and philosophies. Everything I read seemed to make sense when I read it. Eureka! I'd think, that's it. All I need to do to find enlightenment is become macrobiotic, study yoga, eat fruit, meditate, smoke pot, and so on. Now I see life as having so many options and possibilities that I'm not sure whether I am supposed to be here or somewhere else entirely. The fickle finger that pointed out my particular fate has certainly been stuck up some very odd crevasses from time to time.

An example of an odd one resurfaced only a few months before Dad died. I suddenly had a phone call from a man who been an early boyfriend all of forty years ago when I was a member of Ramsgate youth club. I had been very taken with him at the time. He was the cock of the club, so to speak, and bore a strong resemblance to Kirk Douglas. He had emigrated to America, leaving me quite heart-broken, and I hadn't seen him since. Now he was back in Ramsgate on a visit and had tracked me down.

The image of a grey-haired, rugged version of the Kirk Douglas lookalike I had known flashed through my mind, and I took no small pains to make the most of myself before I set out to meet him for a pre-lunch drink in the local pub. But when I entered the bar I could see no one who resembled, even vaguely, my young Lochinvar of yesteryear. Then a voice said, 'Whal, whadda ya know? Neither of us have gotten any younger by the looks of things.'

Perched on a stool, half hidden behind a pillar and beneath a huge Stetson hat, was a small, wizened man wearing a sheepskin coat, bright-blue shirt and bootlace tie, with jeans tucked into high-heeled cowboy boots. I stared at him in disbelief, desperately searching for a trace of the boy he had once been and failing to find one familiar feature in the face before me.

The poor man had been recently widowed. As I was looking through pictures of his children, he produced one of me, a self-conscious stranger sitting on a wall and wearing what was my first two-piece swim suit.

'When Ah showed that picture to ma kids,' he said with a speculative look in his eye, 'Ah told them that if things had turned out differently you might have been their momma.'

Would I? Or would common sense have prevailed long before fate had slipped that ring on my fickle finger?

Sometimes I play mind games, imagining what would have happened if I had taken one small step in another direction. If I had made contact with Tony on that last day. If I had been strong enough to insist that John never took another drink. If I had wasted less time and energy chasing my own tail – or someone else's.

But life is not about what might have been. Life is about what is. All I can hope for in the future is always to live in the present and not make the mistake of falling backwards, because, as Thurber once said, 'It's better to fall flat on your face than to bend over backwards too far.'

All these books are available at your local bookshop or newsagent, or can be ordered direct from the publisher. Indicate the number of copies required and fill in the form below.

Send to: **CS Department, Pan Books Ltd., P.O. Box 40, Basingstoke, Hants. RG21 2YT.**

or phone: 0256 469551 (Ansaphone), quoting title, author and Credit Card number.

Please enclose a remittance* to the value of the cover price plus: 60p for the first book plus 30p per copy for each additional book ordered to a maximum charge of £2.40 to cover postage and packing.

*Payment may be made in sterling by UK personal cheque, postal order, sterling draft or international money order, made payable to Pan Books Ltd.

Alternatively by Barclaycard/Access:

Card No. | | | | | | | | | | | | | | | | | | |

Signature:

Applicable only in the UK and Republic of Ireland.

While every effort is made to keep prices low, it is sometimes necessary to increase prices at short notice. Pan Books reserve the right to show on covers and charge new retail prices which may differ from those advertised in the text or elsewhere.

NAME AND ADDRESS IN BLOCK LETTERS PLEASE:

....

Name ————————————————————————

Address ———————————————————————

————————————————————————————

————————————————————————————

————————————————————————————

3/87